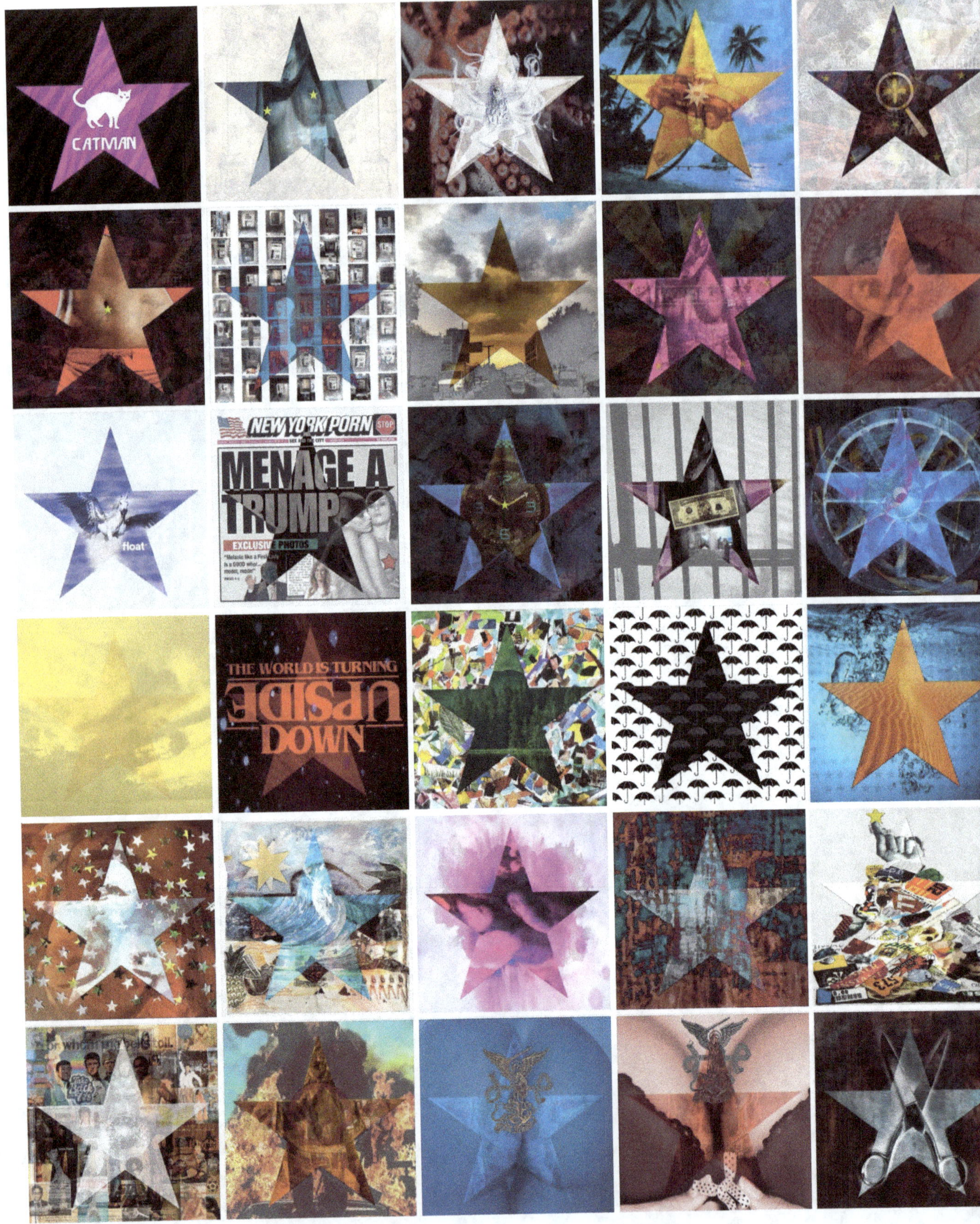

Februllage 2022

Februllage 2022

First edition: May 2022

Primera edición: Mayo 2022

© **2022. Fabián Giles.**

Design & Photography

Diseño y Fotografía:

FABIÁN GILES

www.facebook.com/FabianGilesArt

www.instagram.com/fabiangiles

Printed by

amazon publishing

Impreso por

All Rights Reserved. Any reproduction by any mechanical or electronic media is only with written autorization by the author.

Todos los derechos reservados. La reproducción por cualquier medio mecánico o electrónico es con la autorización escrita del autor.

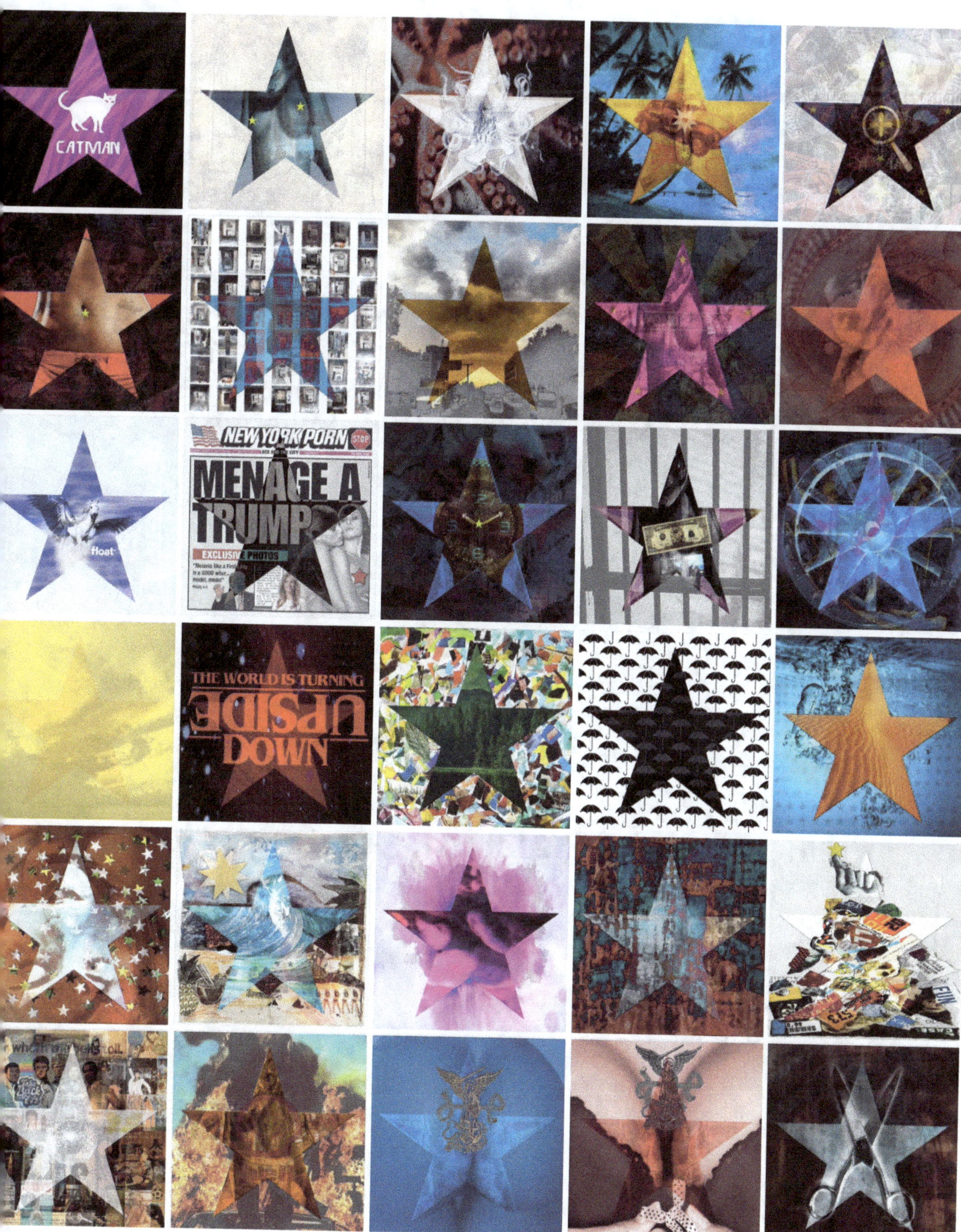
CATMAN
NEW YORK PORN
MENAGE A TRUMP
EXCLUSIVE PHOTOS
THE WORLD IS TURNING
UPSIDE DOWN

Februllage

Official 2022 Prompt List in **English**
Our challenge

1st February
Cat

2nd February
Sisters

3rd February
Octopus

4th February
Escape

5th February
Magnifying Glass

6th February
Overdress

7th February
Telephone

8th February
Clouds

9th February
Surprise

10th February
Disturbing

11th February
Float

12th February
Newspaper

13th February
Time

14th February
Stolen

15th February
Wheel

16th February
Calm

17th February
Upside down

18th February
Forest

19th February
Umbrella

20th February
Thirst

21st February
Hide & Seek

22nd February
Waves

23rd February
Ink

24th February
Stack

25th February
1970's

26th February
Fire

27th February
Climb

28th February
Scissors

Enjoy!

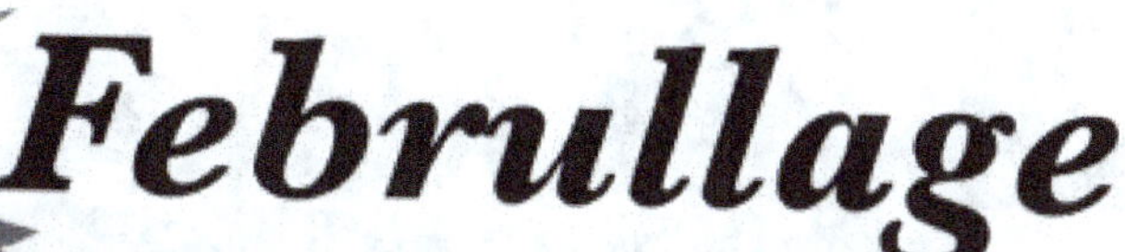

Februllage
Official 2022 Prompt List Spanish
Our challenge

1st February
Gato

2nd February
Hermana

3rd February
Pulpo

4th February
Escape

5th February
Lupa

6th February
vestirse en exceso

7th February
Teléfono

8th February
Nube

9th February
Sorpresa

10th February
Perturbador

11th February
Flotar

12th February
Periódico

13th February
Tiempo

14th February
Robado

15th February
Llanta

16th February
Calma

17th February
Boca abajo

18th February
Bosque

19th February
Sombrilla

20th February
Sed

21st February
Escondidas

22nd February
Olas

23rd February
Tinta

24th February
Pila

25th February
1970

26th February
Fuego

27th February
Trepar

28th February
Tijeras

Enjoy!

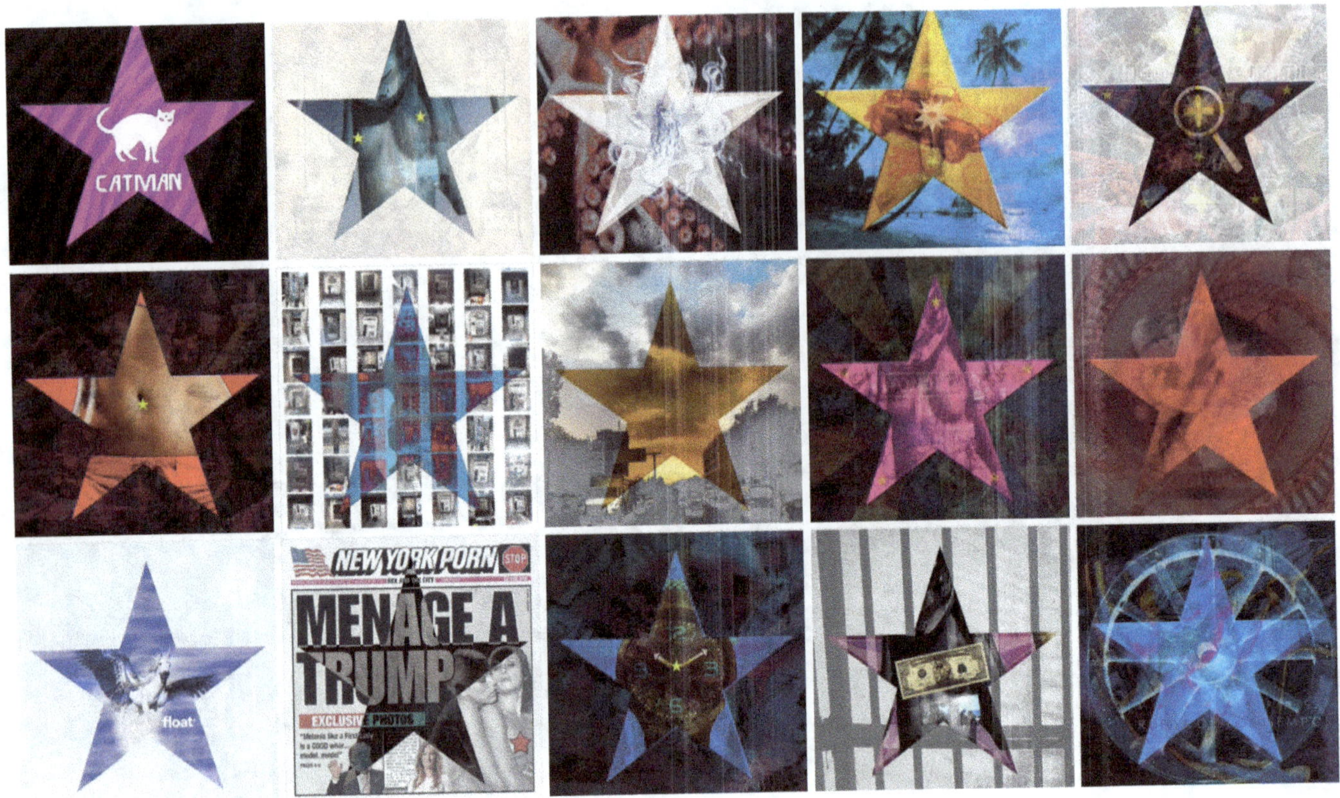

Februllage 2022

This is an INSTAGRAM based project only which is a collaboration between Edinburgh Collage Collective and the Scandinavian Collage Museum.

FEBRULLAGE How To:

1. Make a collage based on the daily prompt (analog or digital)

2. Post it on instagram

3. Instagram hashtag it with #februllage and #februllage2022

You can set your own goals. For example, this can be one collage a day or three a week... the decision is entirely yours! Importantly, **Februllage** is about fun and collage creativity and cutouts, inspiration and practice, dedication and challenge, it's for you!

Everyday will showcase on our INSTAGRAM feed a selection of the collages made that day. There are many more made than we are able to show here. Please take a look at all the amazing work by searching the hashtags #februllage #februllage2022

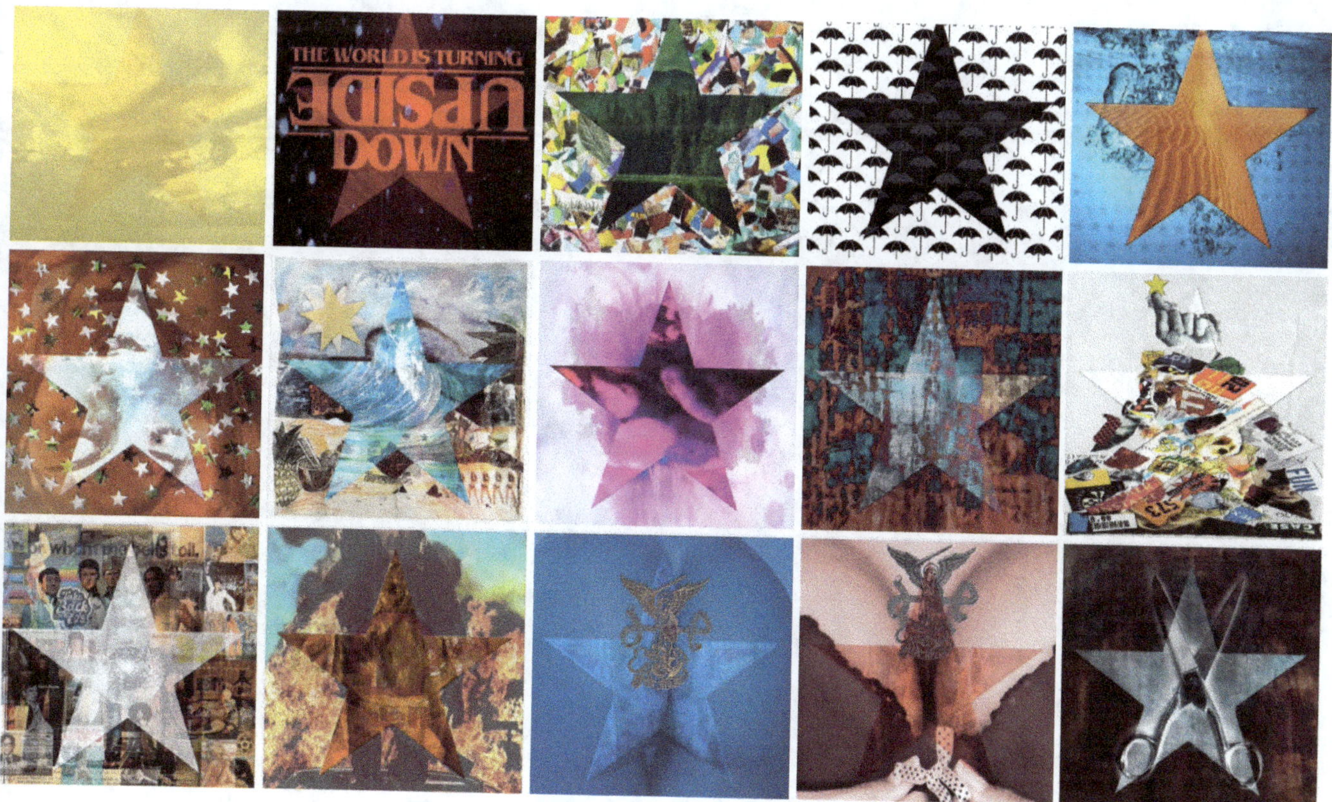

Februllage 2022

Este es un proyecto basado únicamente en INSTAGRAM el cual es una colaboración entre el Colectivo de Collage de Edinburgo y el Museo de Collage Escandinavo.

FEBRULLAGE. Cómo hacerlo:

1. Hacer un collage basado en el tema del día (analogo o digital)

2. Postearlo en Instagram

3. Usar el hashtag #februllage y #februllage2022

Pueden fijar sus propias metas. Por ejemplo, este puede ser un collage por día o tres por semana... la decisión es suya.   Lo más importante, **Februllage** se trata de diversión y creatividad y recortes de collage, de inspiración y práctica, dedicación y desafío, ¡es para todos!

Cada día se muestra en INSTAGRAM una selección de los collages hechos durante el día. Hay muchos más de los que podemos mostrar aquí. Por favor, echen un vistazo a todo el increíble trabajo buscando los hashtags #februllage #februllage2022

Februllage 2022

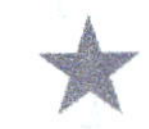

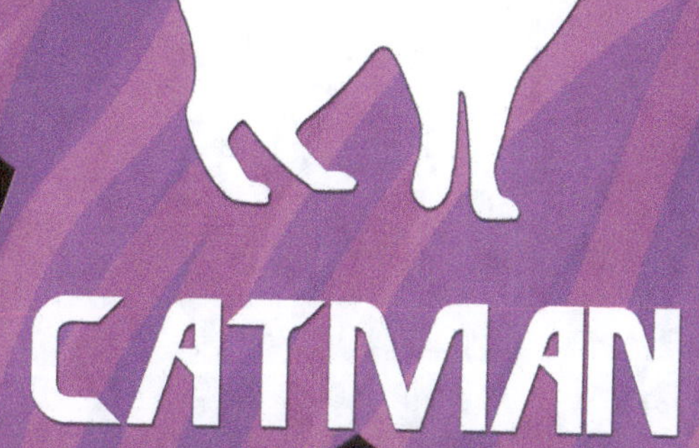

CATMAN

Februllage 2022

2 Sisters of Mercy
Mixed Media
Técnica Mixta
Feb 2022

FABIÁN GILES

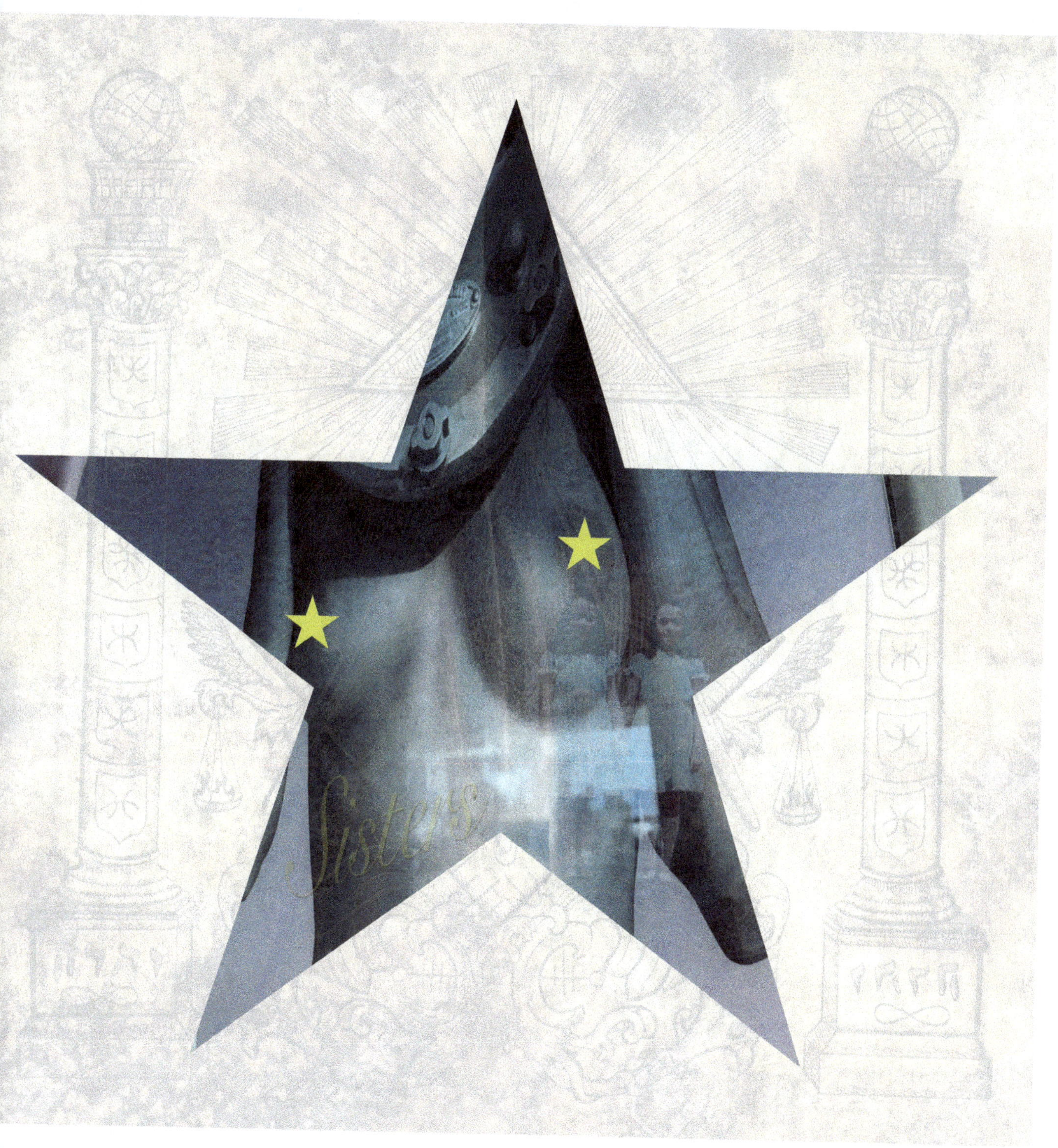
Sisters

Februllage 2022

Mixed Media
Técnica Mixta
Feb 2022

FABIÁN GILES

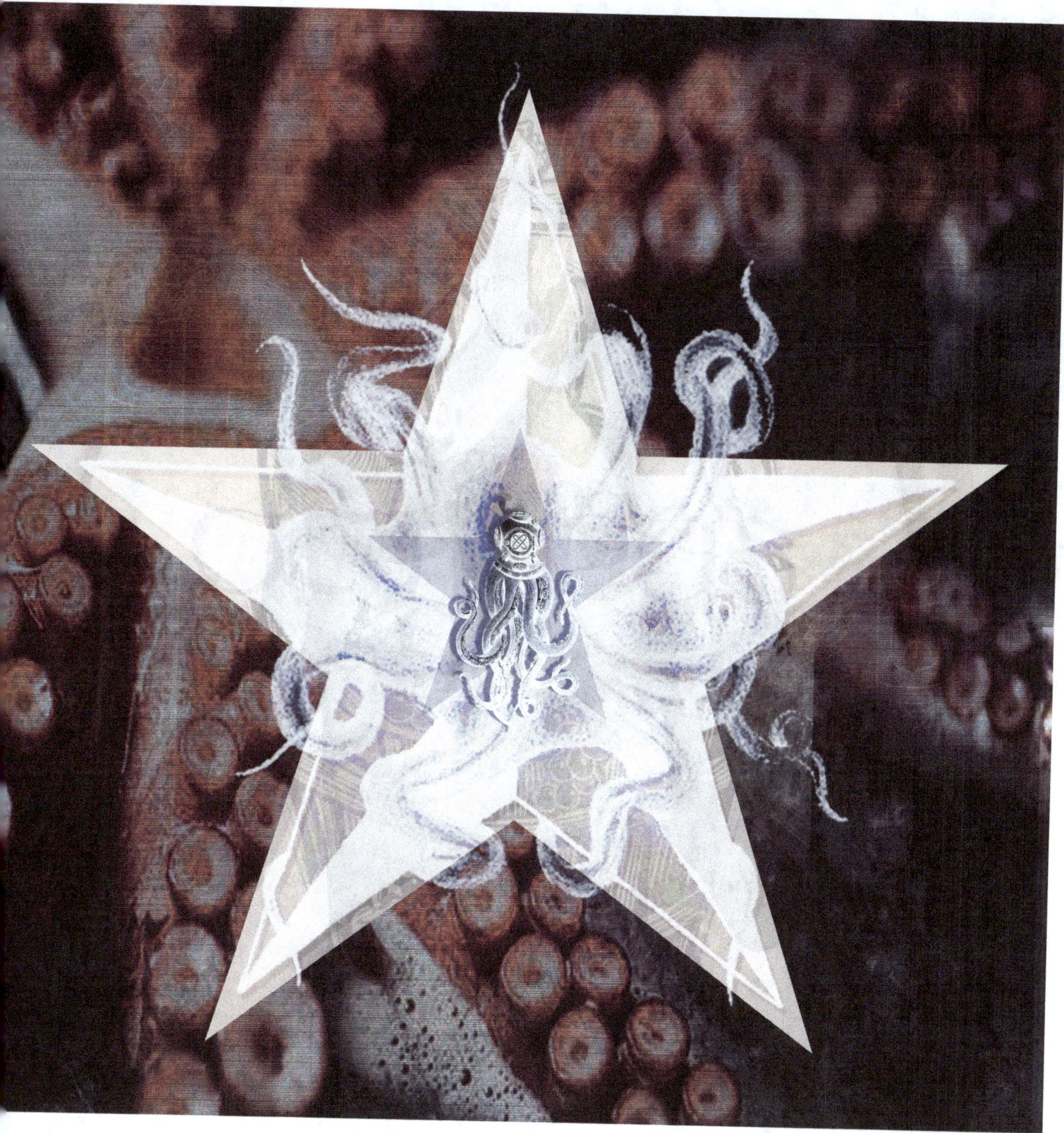

Februllage 2022

Mixed Media
Técnica Mixta
Feb 2022

FABIÁN GILES

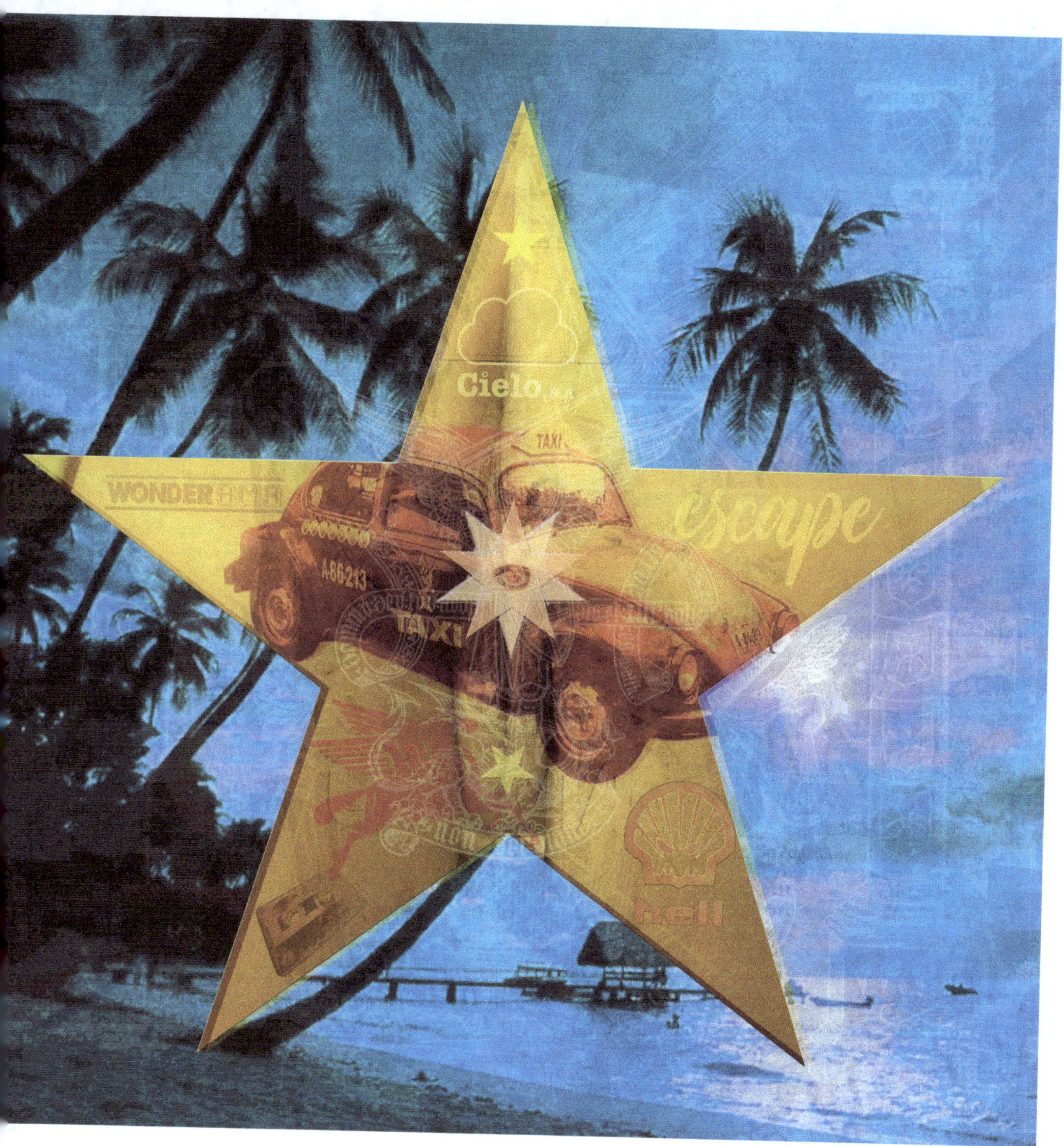

Cielo s.a.
WONDER
escape
TAXI
TAXI
A 86213
Shell
bell

Februllage 2022

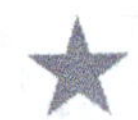

5 Zoom to more positive
Mixed Media
Técnica Mixta
Feb 2022

FABIÁN GILES

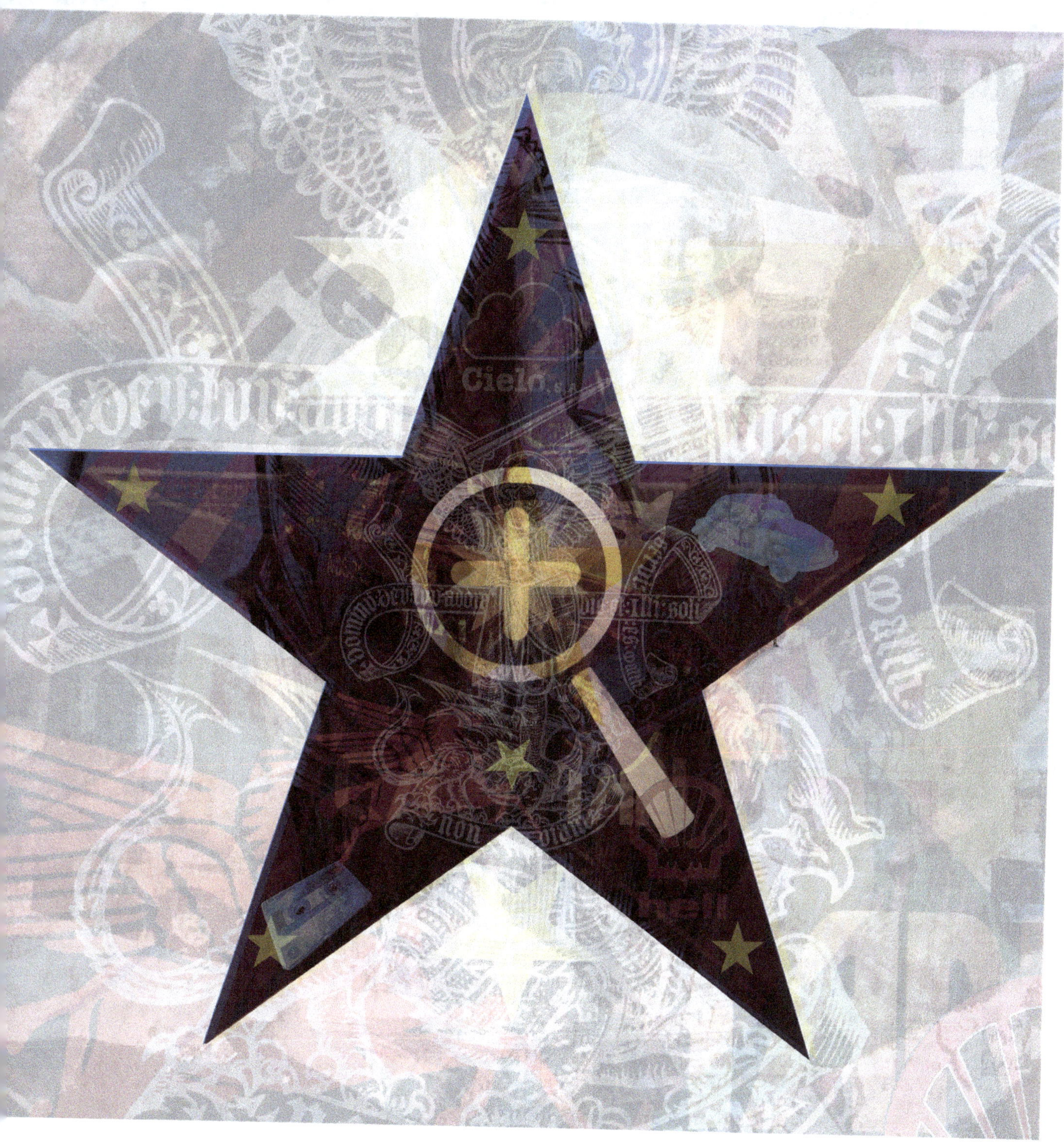

Februllage 2022

6 Overdressed
Mixed Media
Técnica Mixta
Feb 2022

FABIÁN GILES

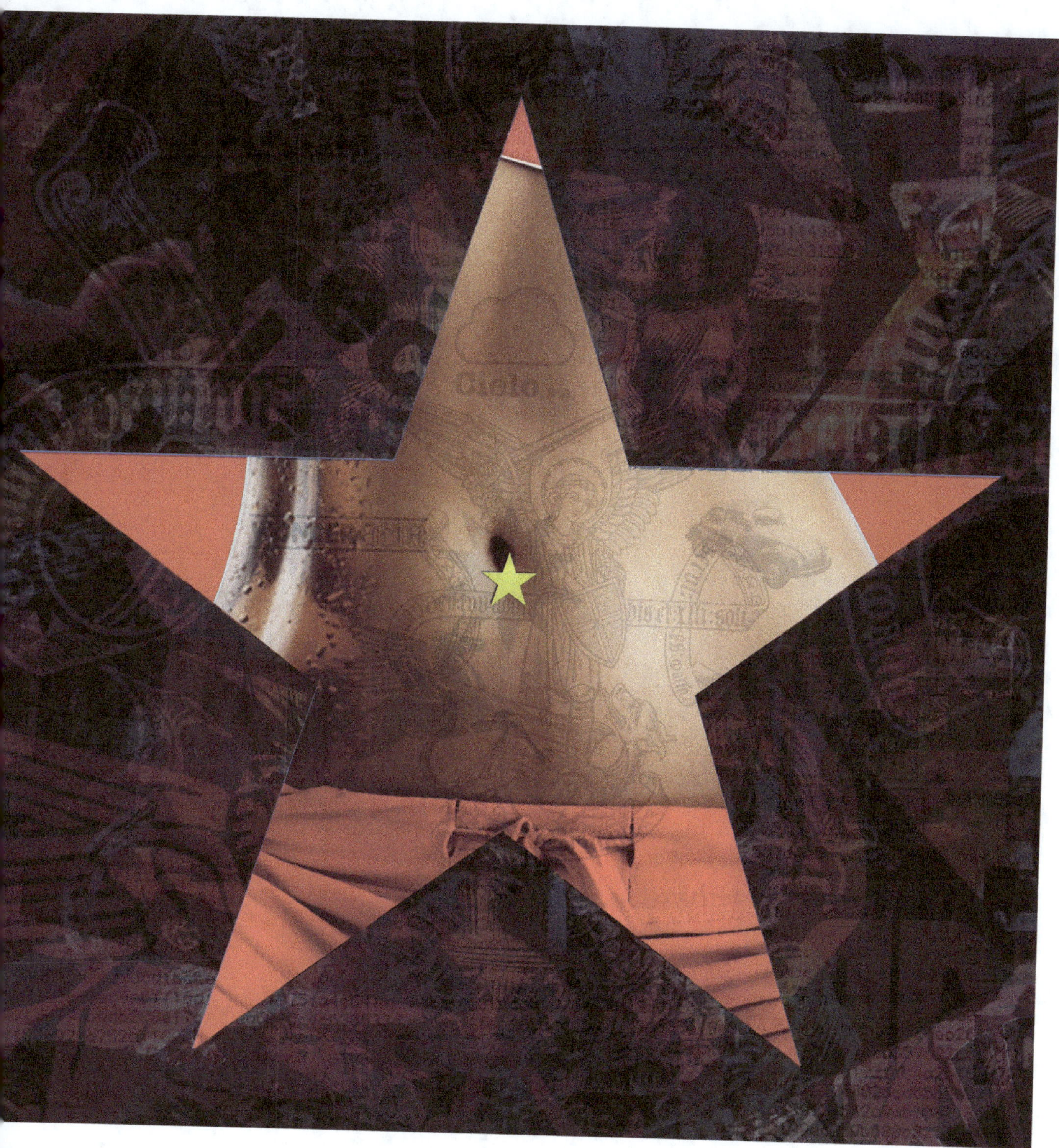

Cielo...

Februllage 2022

7 Telephones
Mixed Media
Técnica Mixta
Feb 2022

FABIÁN GILES

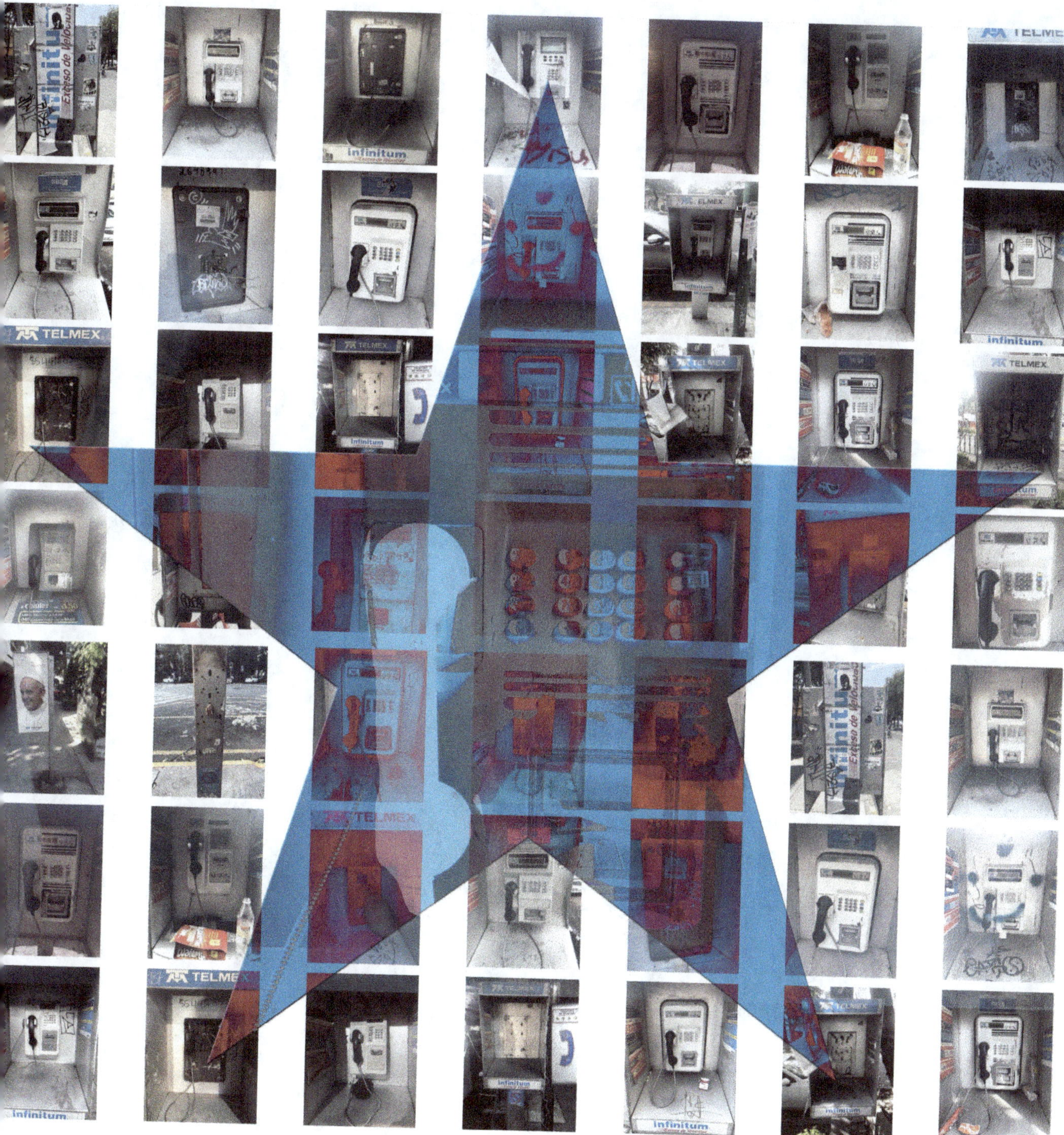

Februllage 2022

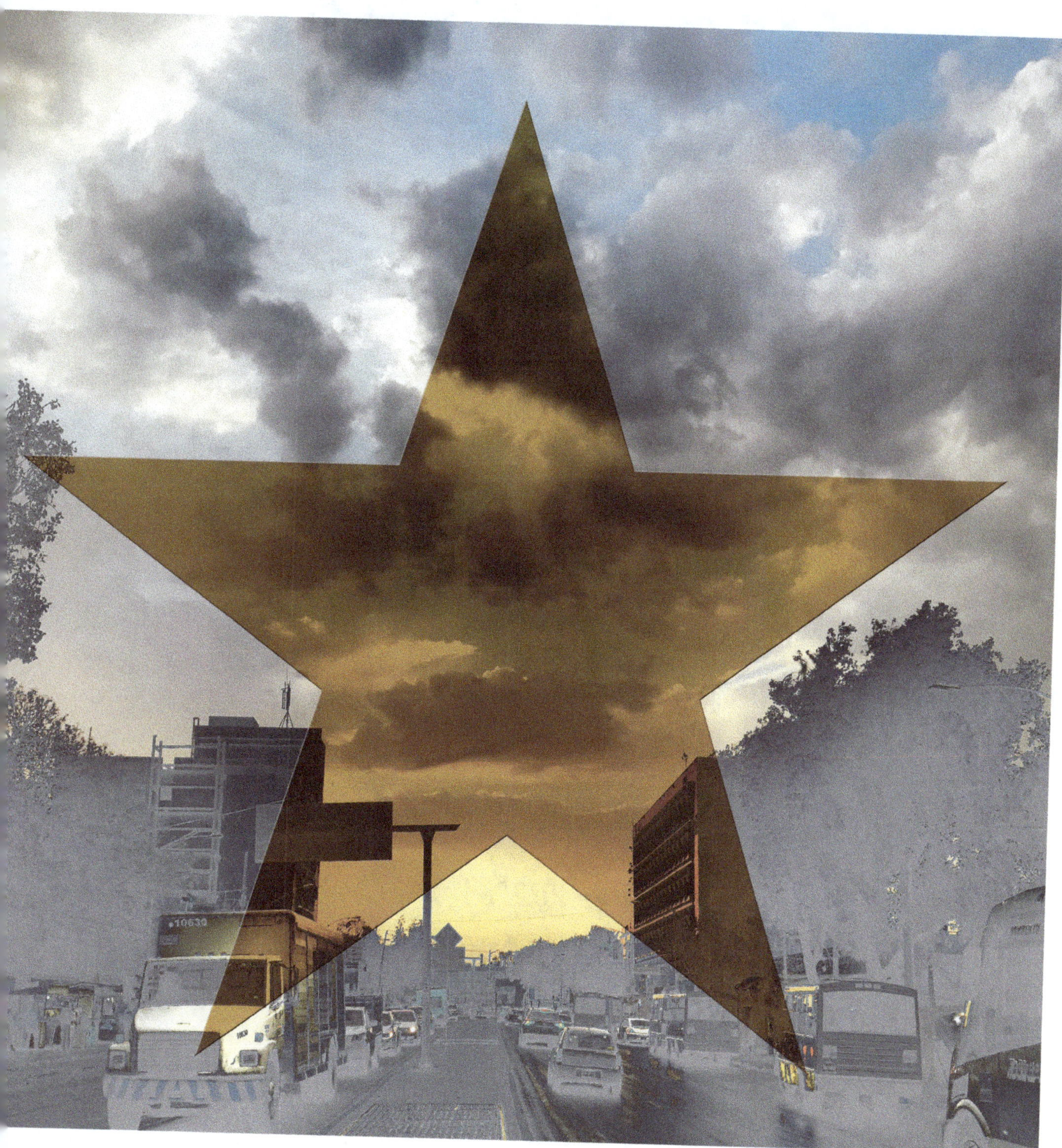

Februllage 2022

FABIÁN GILES

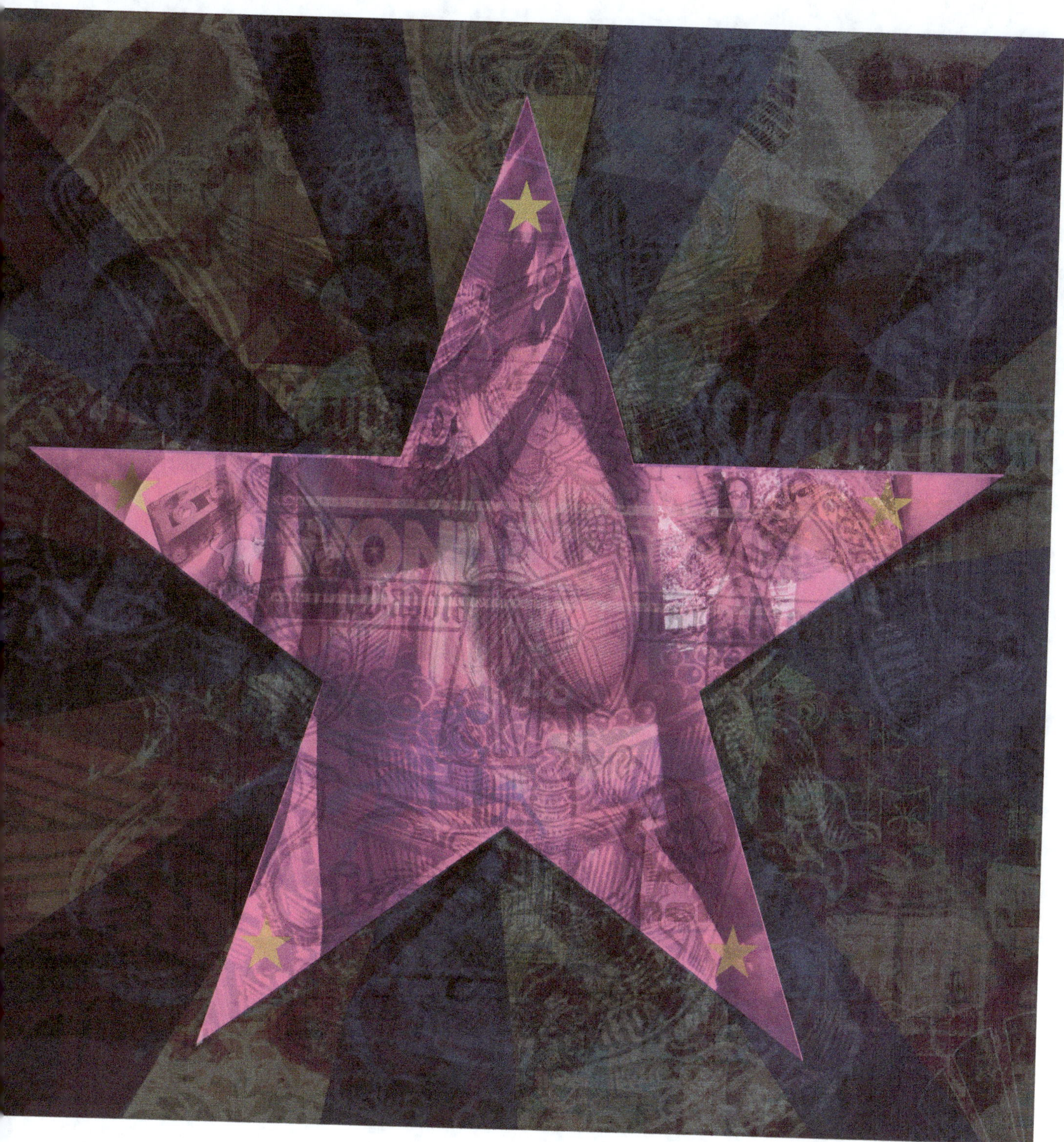

Februllage 2022

10 Disturbed
Mixed Media
Técnica Mixta
Feb 2022

FABIÁN GILES

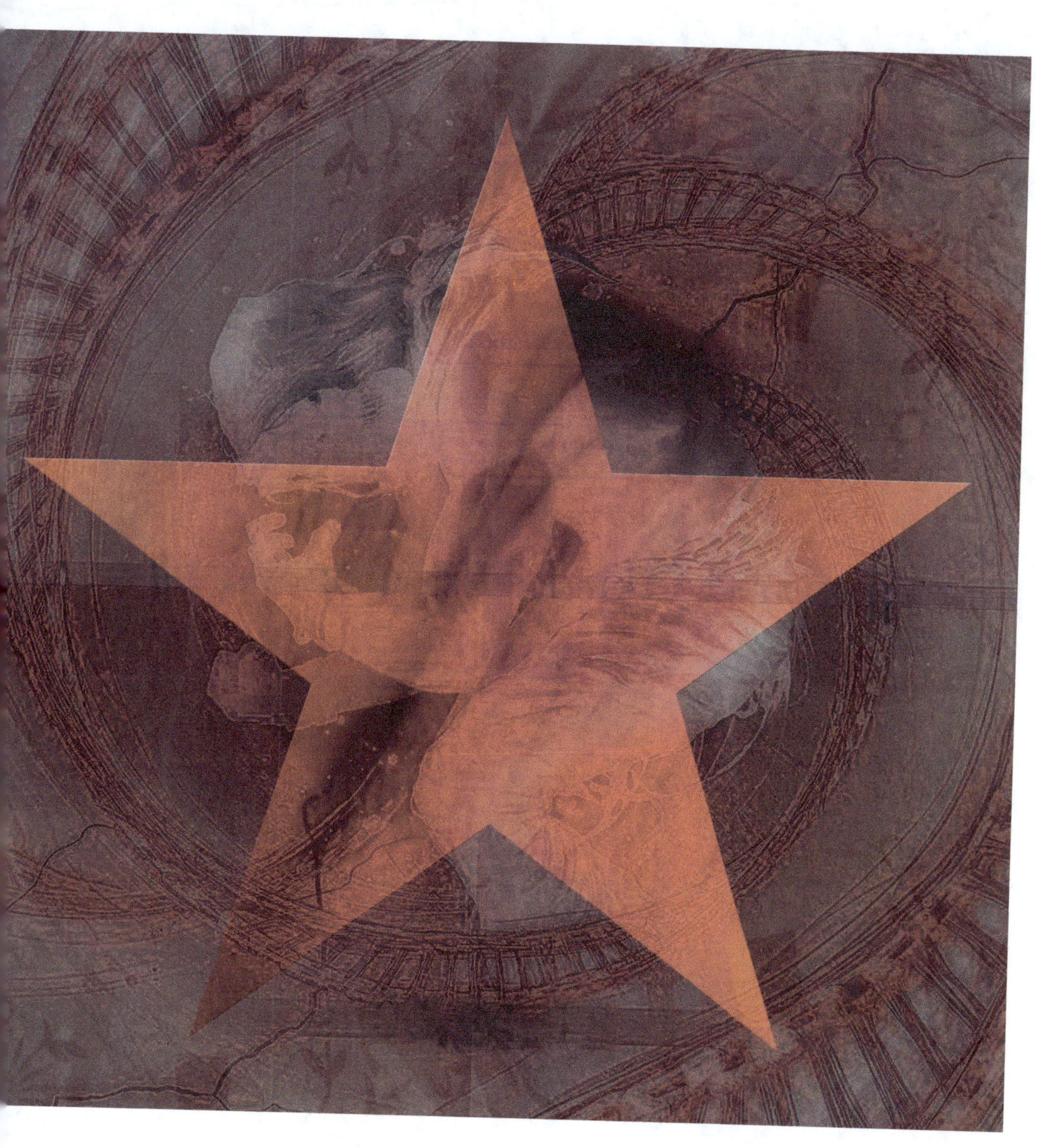

Februllage 2022

11 Float
Mixed Media
Técnica Mixta
Feb 2022

FABIÁN GILES

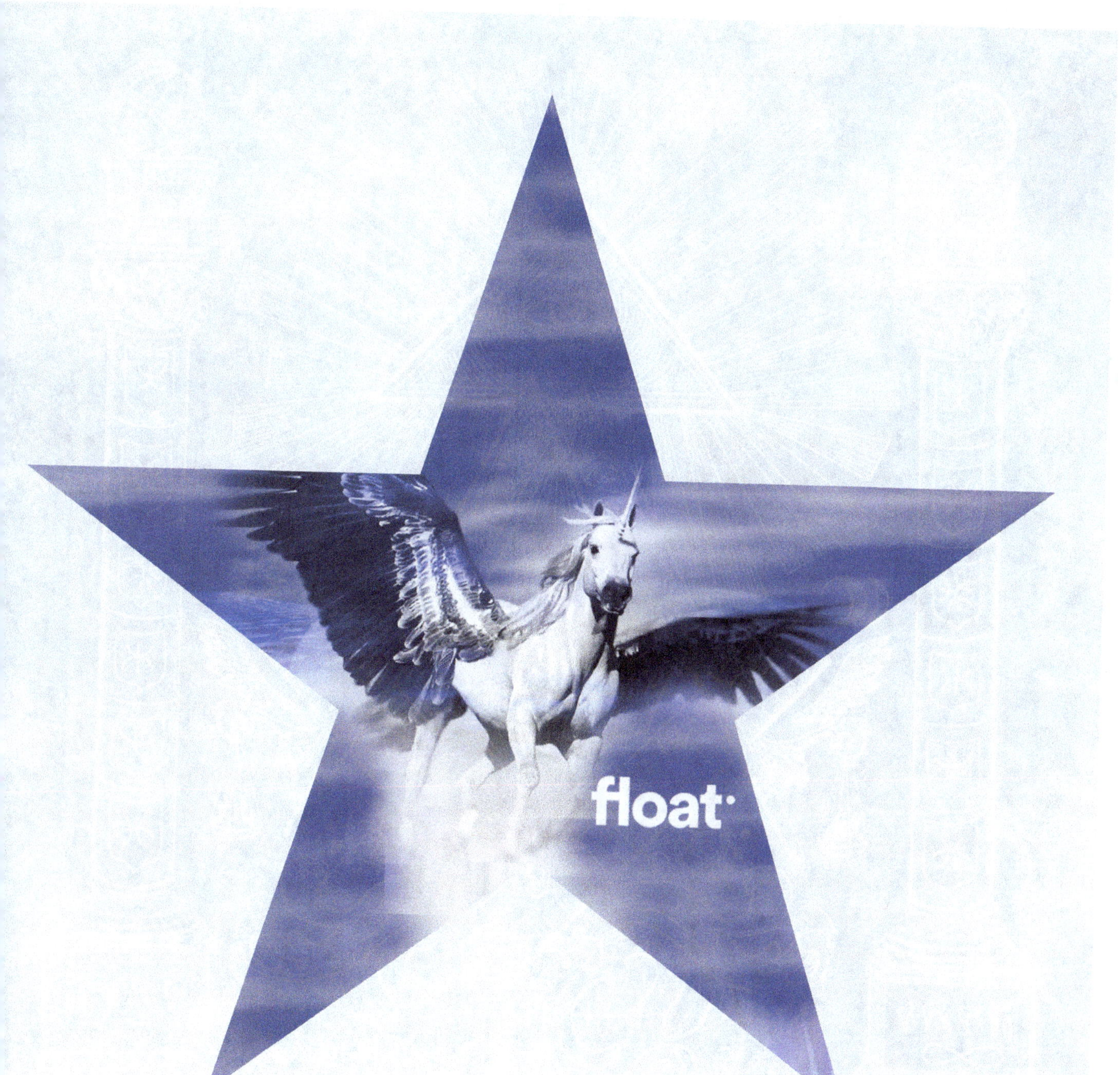

float·

Februllage 2022

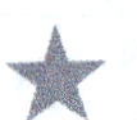

Mixed Media
Técnica Mixta
Feb 2022

FABIÁN GILES

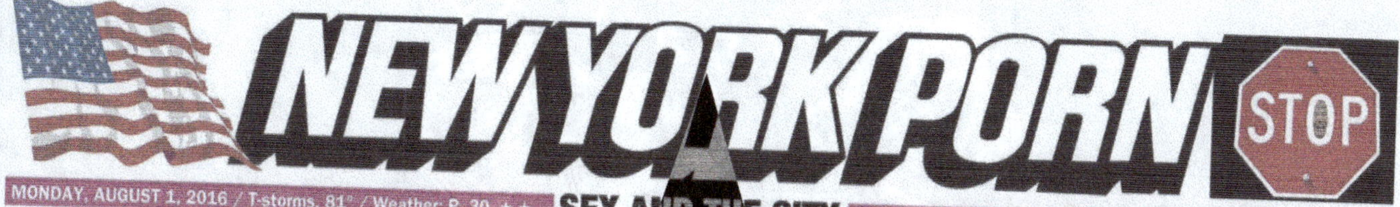

MONDAY, AUGUST 1, 2016 / T-storms, 81° / Weather: P. 30 ★ ★   SEX AND THE CITY   nyporn.com $1'000,000

MENAGE A TRUMP

PENTHOUSE / HUSTLER

EXCLUSIVE PHOTOS

"Melania like a First Lady is a GOOD whor... model, model"

PAGES 4-5

Melania Trump had an impressive body of work long before she met The Donald. Then a 25-year-old model, Melania Knauss (far right) posed for a series of sizzling shots with a Scandinavian beauty.

"They're a celebration of the human body as art," a Trump spokesman said.

Februllage 2022

13 TimeWatch
Mixed Media
Técnica Mixta
Feb 2022

FABIÁN GILES

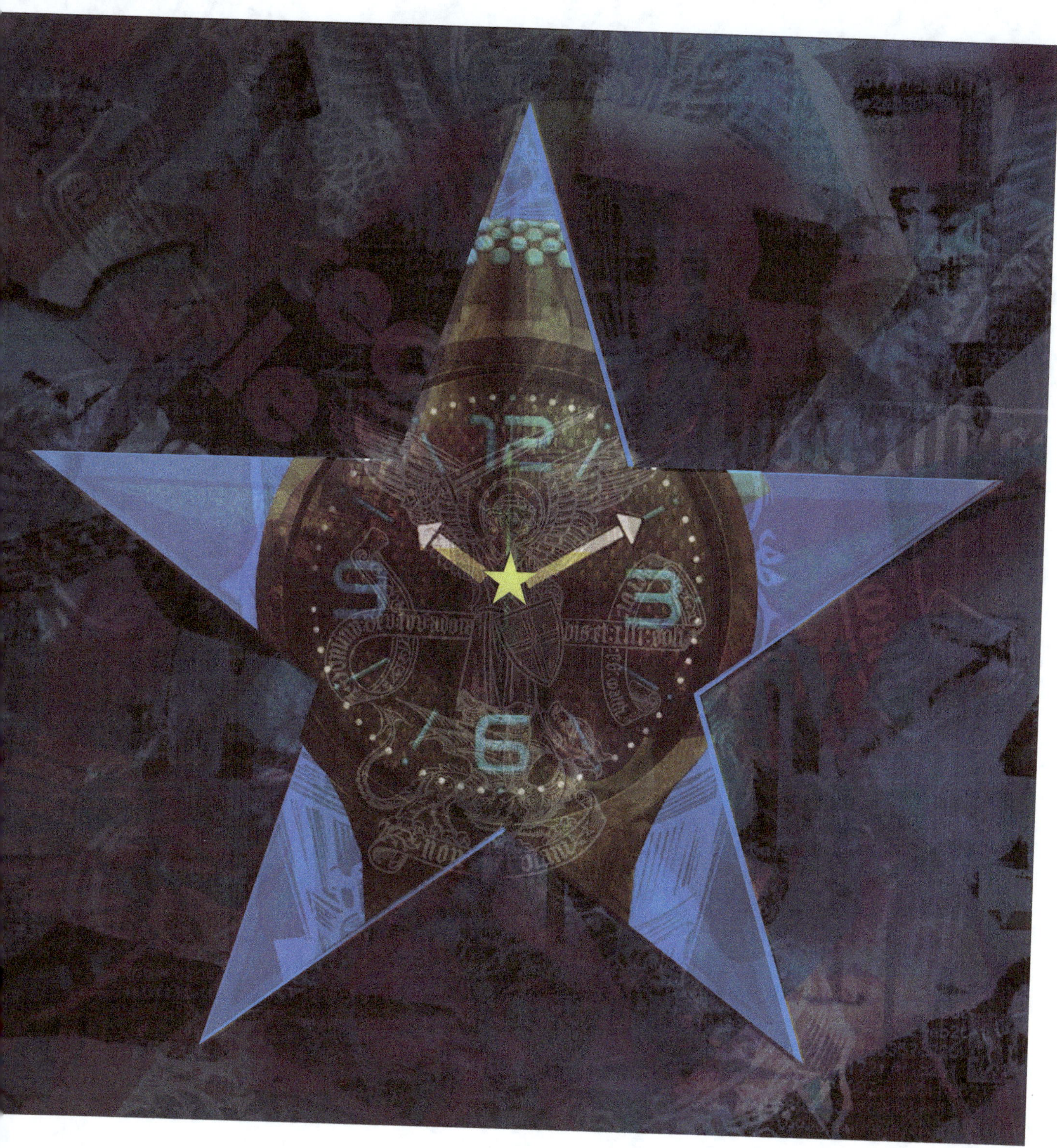

Februllage 2022

14 Jailed
Mixed Media
Técnica Mixta
Feb 2022

FABIÁN GILES

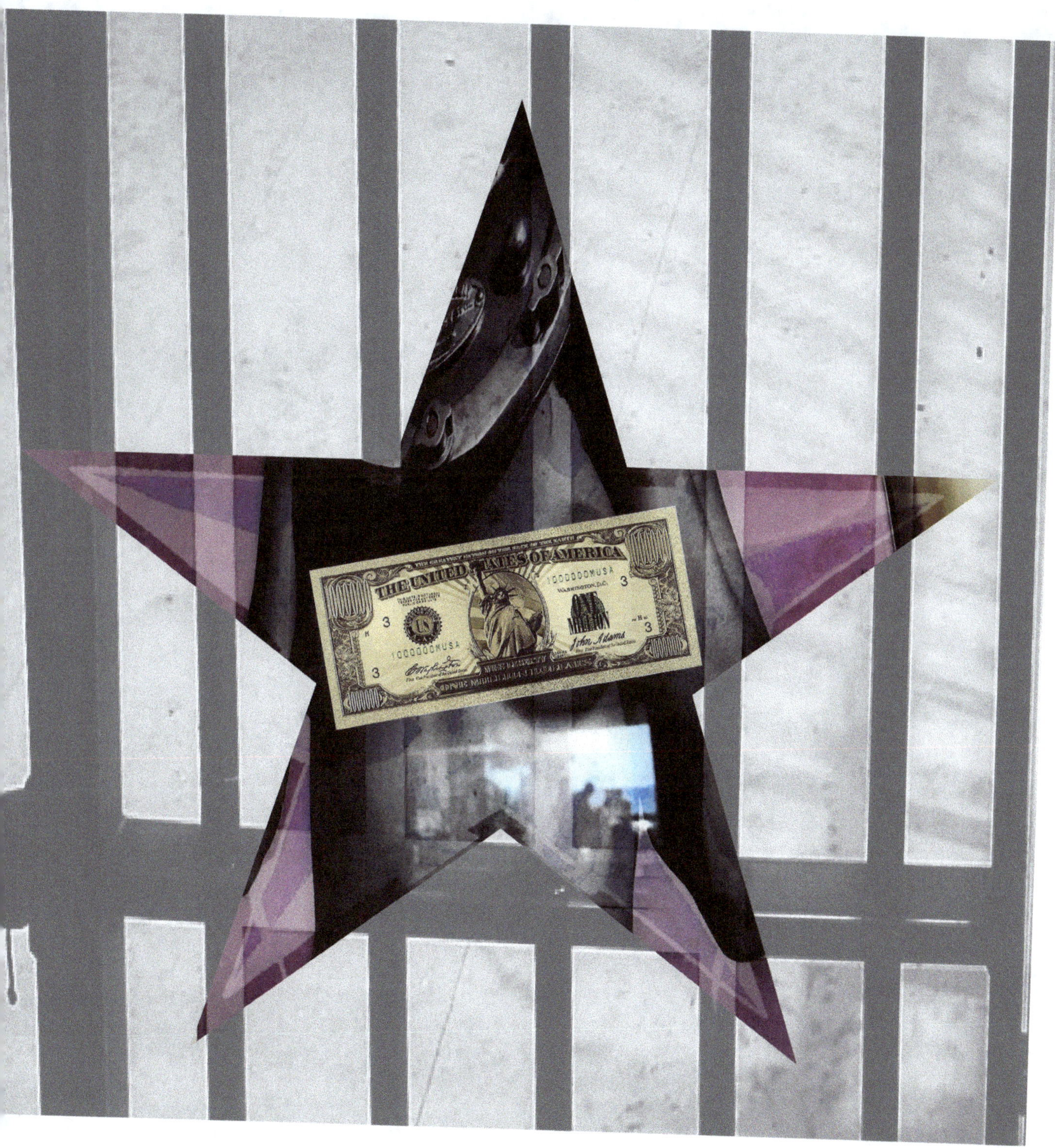

15 Rueda de los Tiempos (revisited)
Mixed Media
Técnica Mixta
Feb 2022

FABIÁN GILES

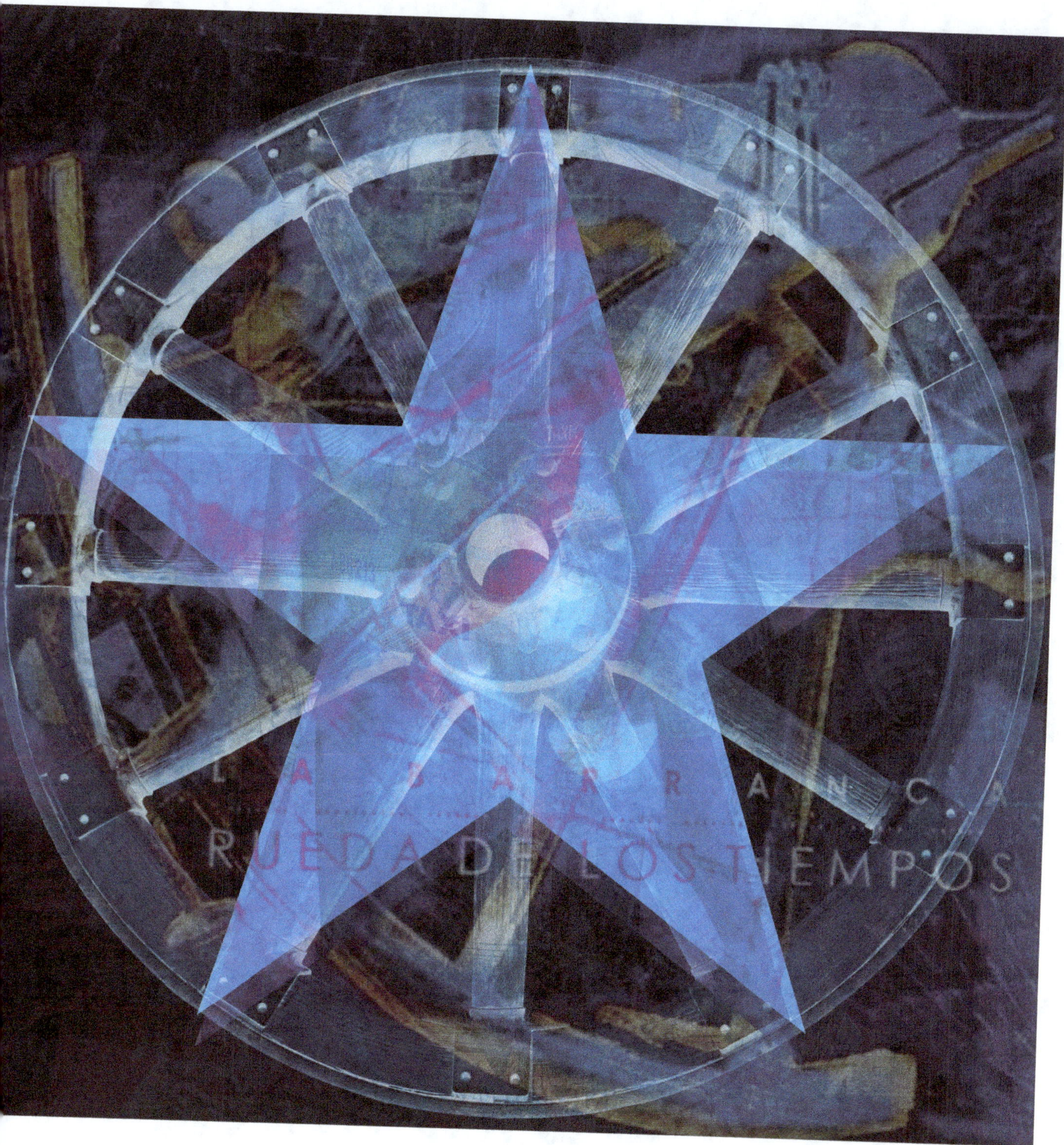

LA BARRANCA
RUEDA DE LOS TIEMPOS

Februllage 2022

16 Calma
Mixed Media
Técnica Mixta
Feb 2022

FABIÁN GILES

Februllage 2022

FABIÁN GILES

THE WORLD IS TURNING
UPSIDE
DOWN

Februllage 2022

18 El Rasicomarma (revisited)
Mixed Media
Técnica Mixta
Feb 2022

FABIÁN GILES

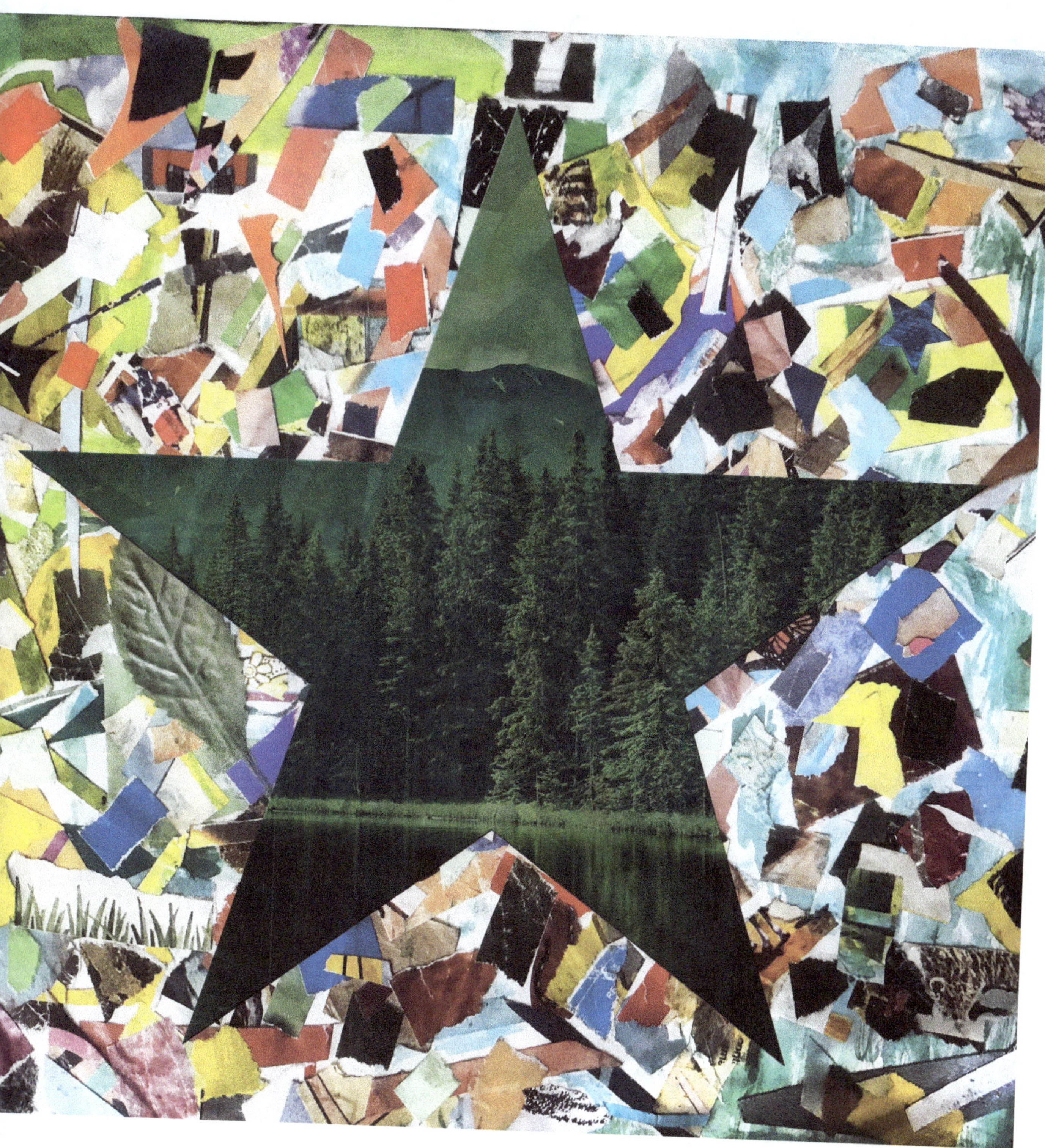

Februllage 2022

19 Umbrellas
Mixed Media
Técnica Mixta
Feb 2022

FABIÁN GILES

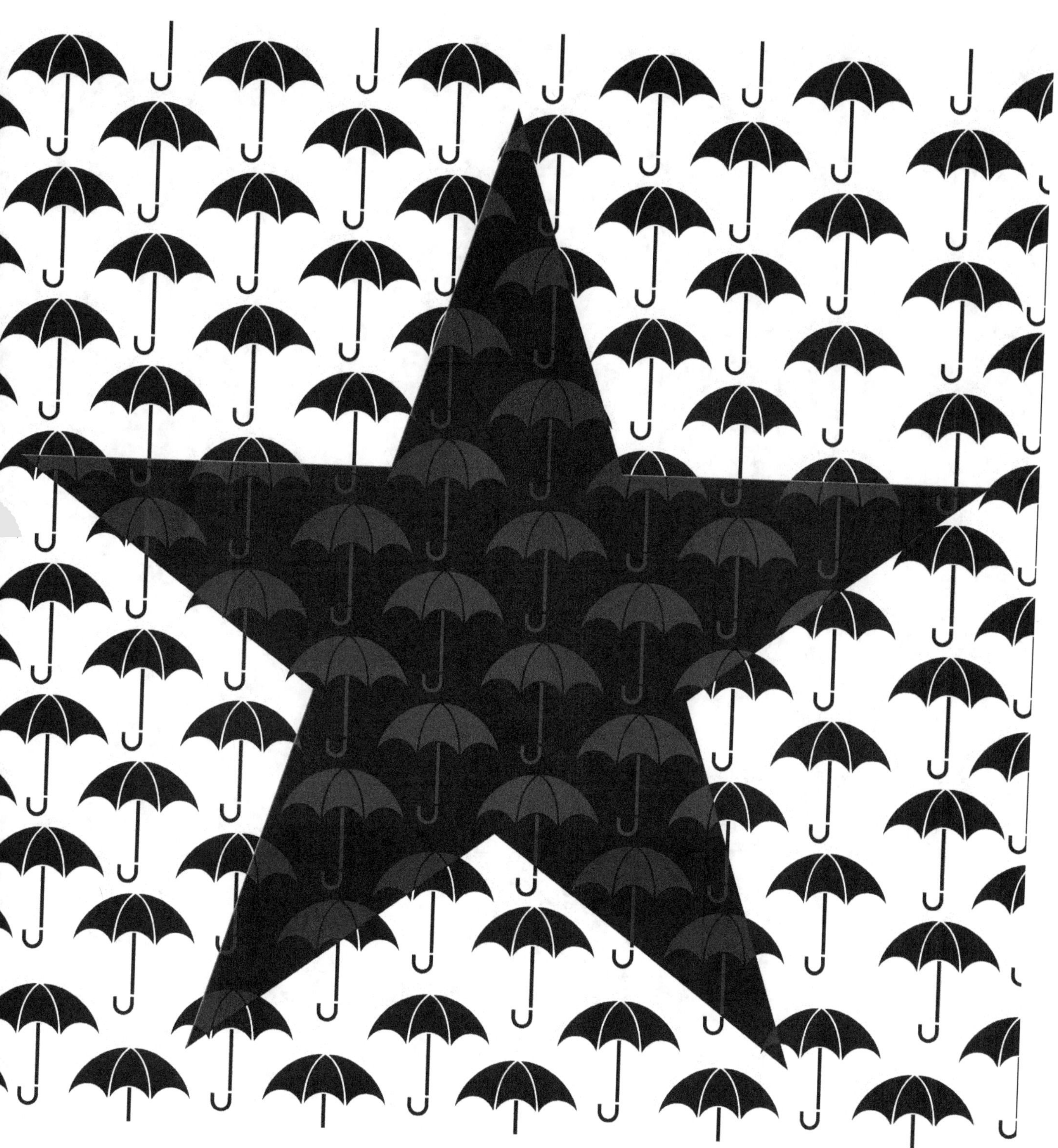

Februllage 2022

Mixed Media
Técnica Mixta
Feb 2022

FABIÁN GILES

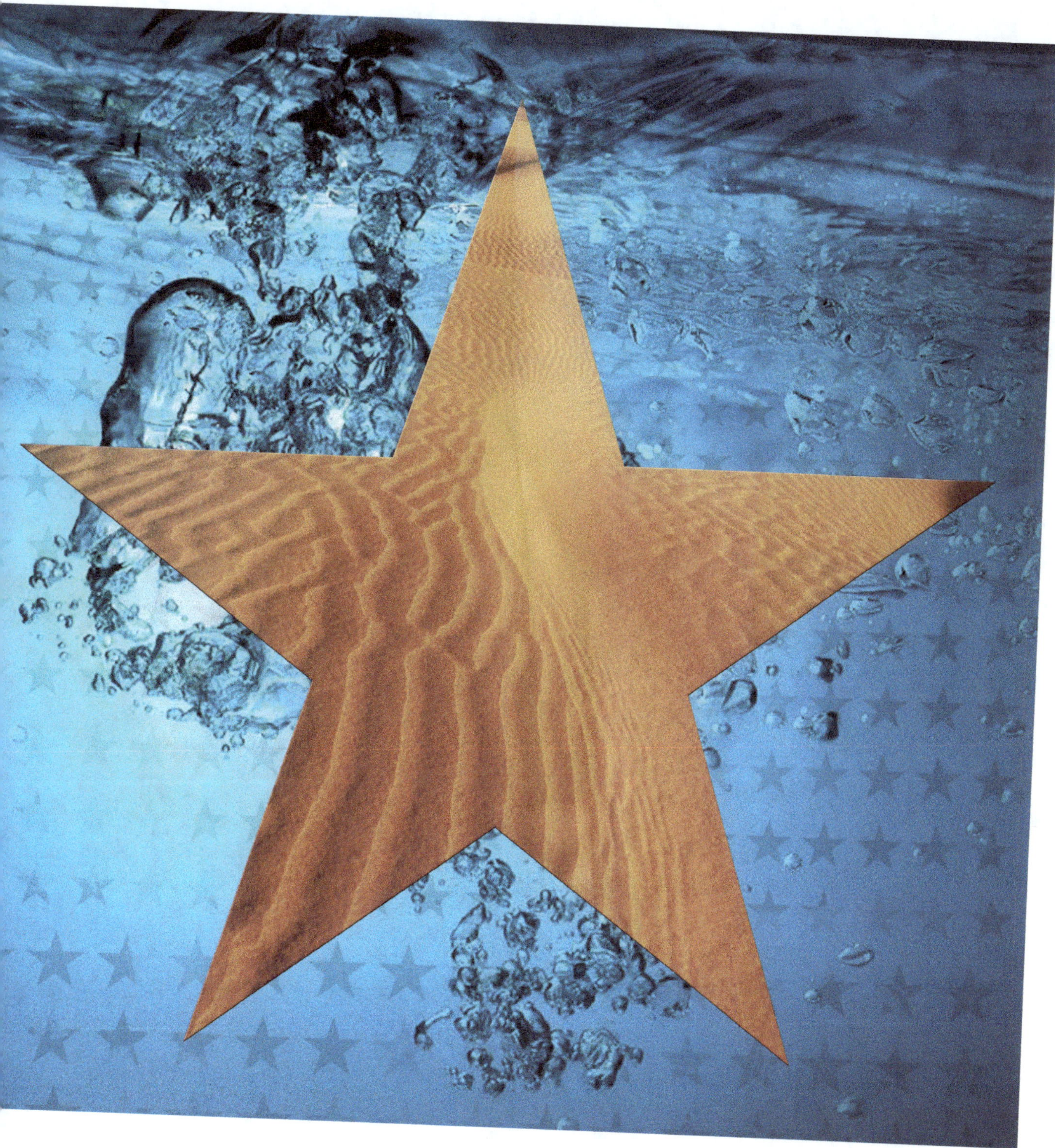

Februllage 2022

21 Escondidas
Mixed Media
Técnica Mixta
Feb 2022

FABIÁN GILES

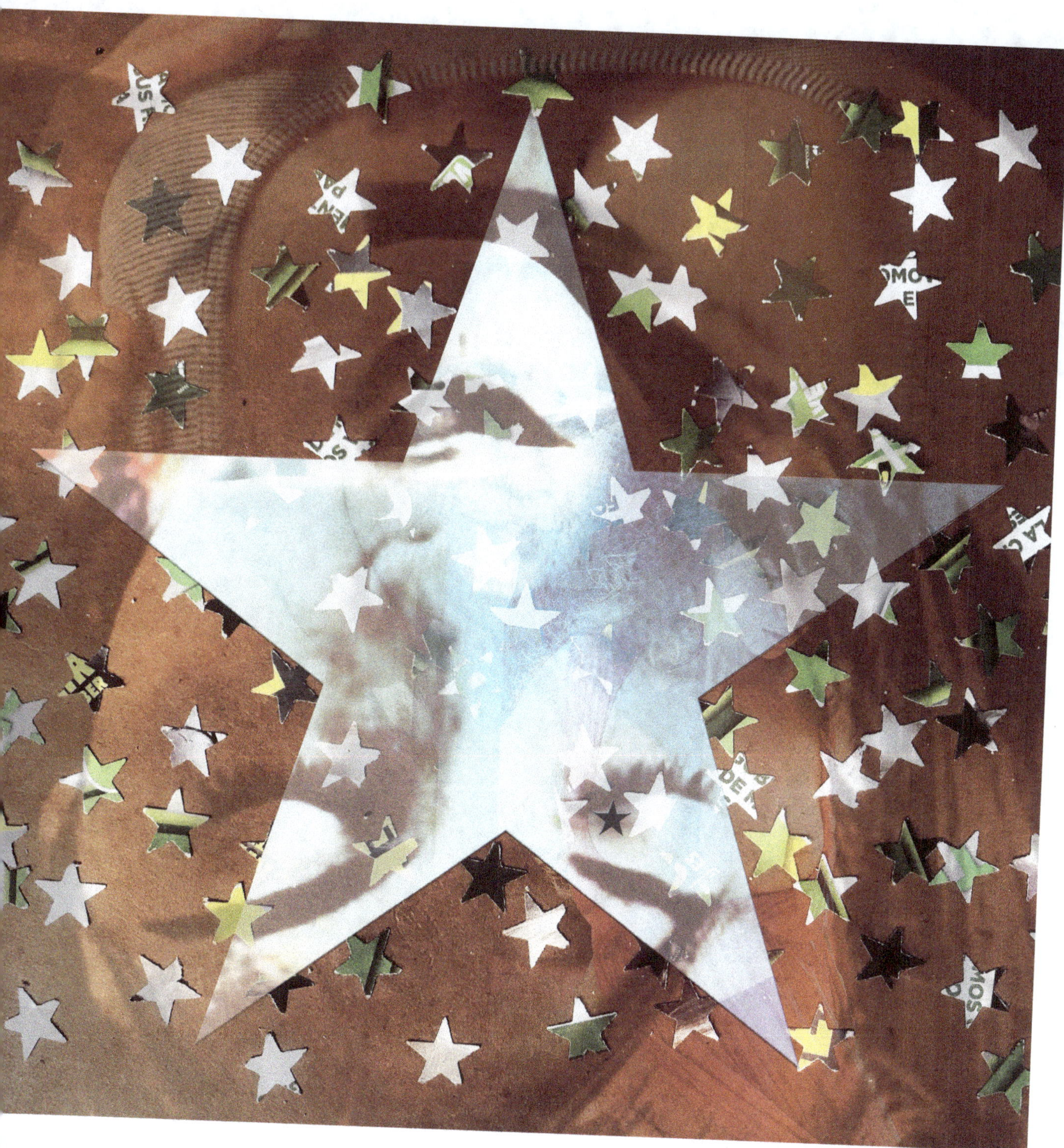

Februllage 2022

22 Sea (revisited)
Mixed Media
Técnica Mixta
Feb 2022

FABIÁN GILES

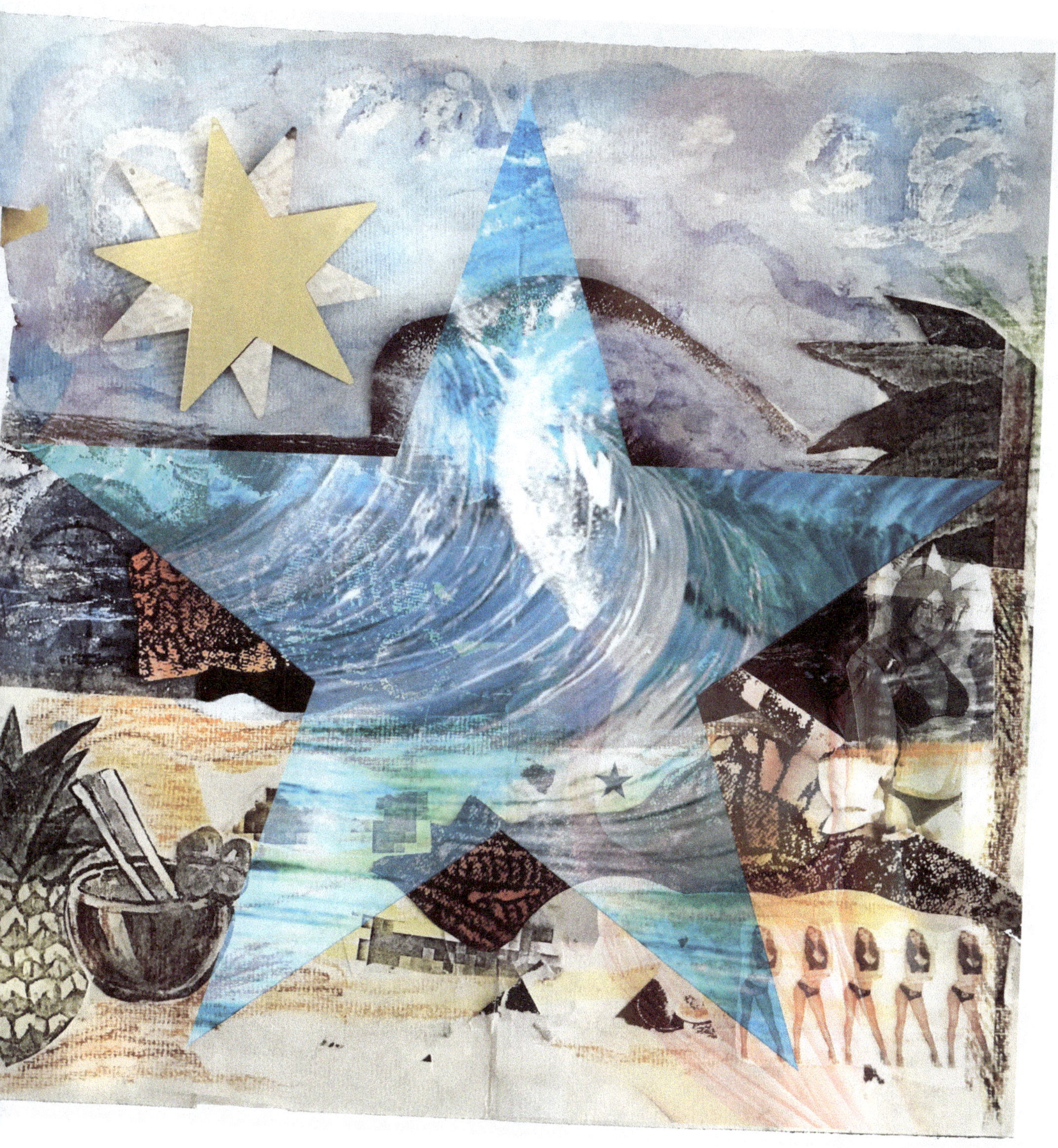

Februllage 2022

23 Mancha
Mixed Media
Técnica Mixta
Feb 2022

FABIÁN GILES

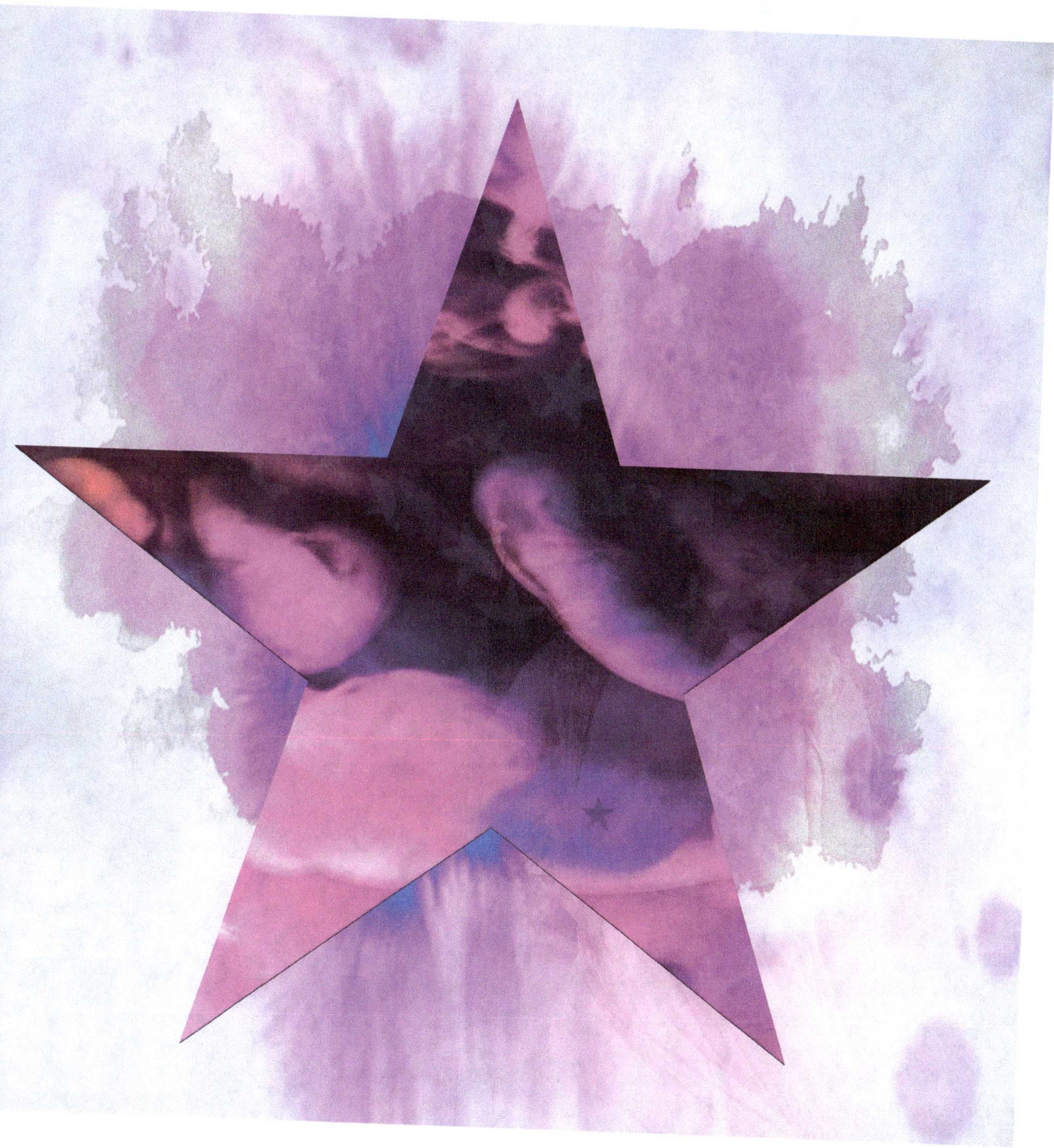

Februllage 2022

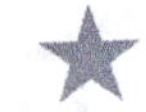

24 Montón
Mixed Media
Técnica Mixta
Feb 2022

FABIÁN GILES

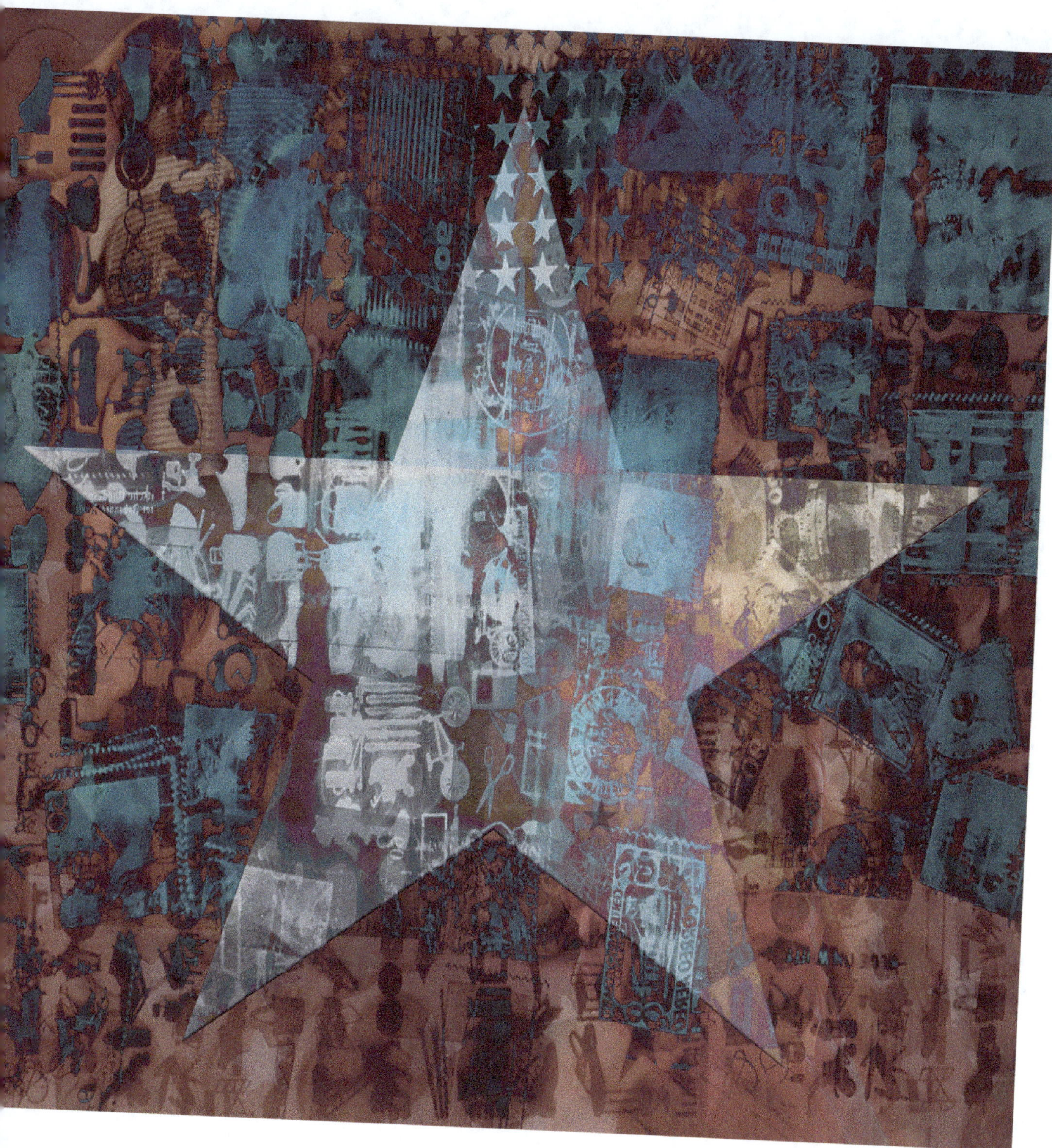

Februllage 2022

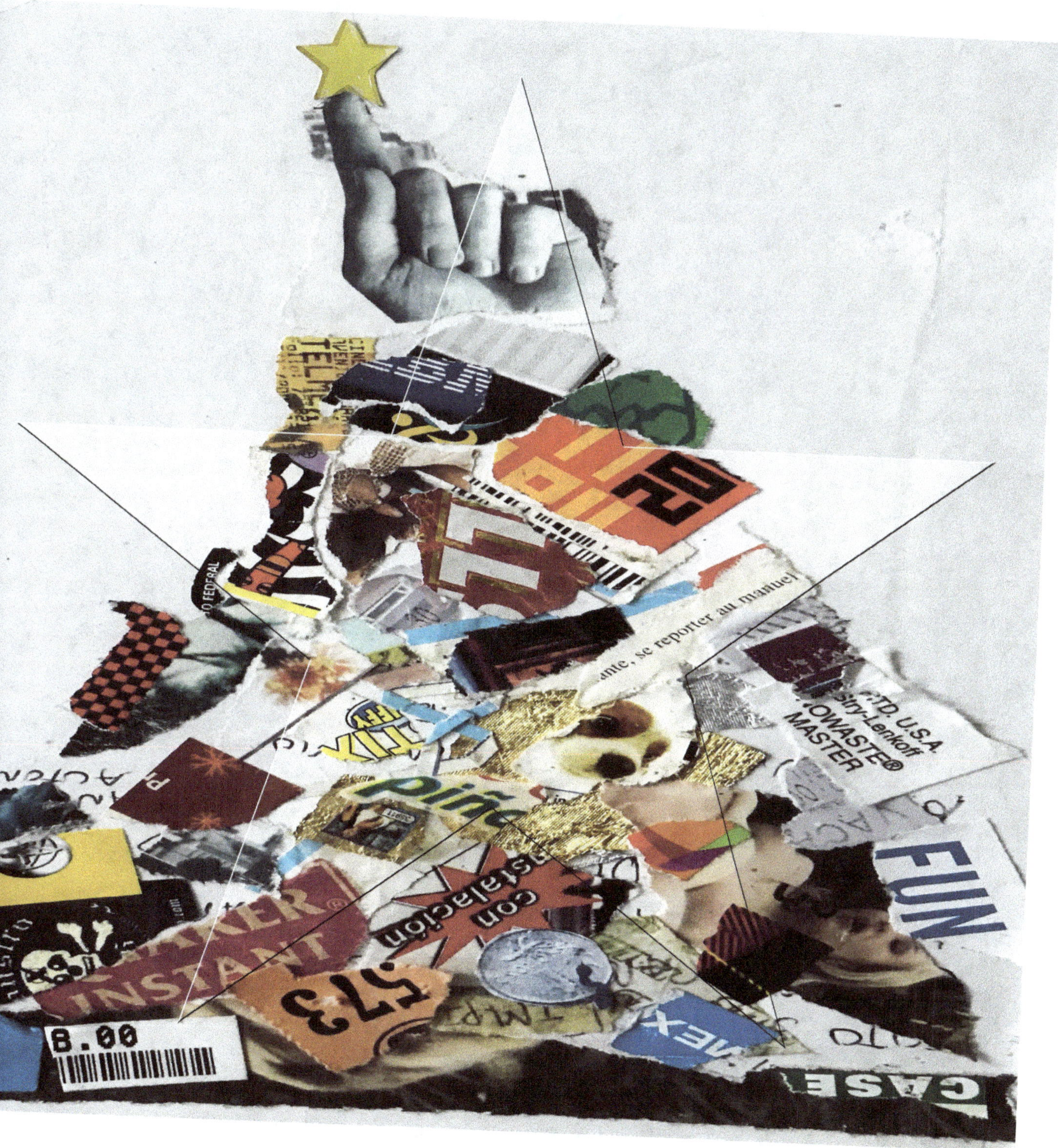

TEL
FUN
FUN
CASE
MEX
INSTANT
513
B.00
piña
con instalación
ante, se reporter au manuel
LTD. U.S.A.
NOWASTE
MASTER
FEDERAL

Februllage 2022

25 70′s

Mixed Media
Técnica Mixta
Feb 2022
FABIÁN GILES

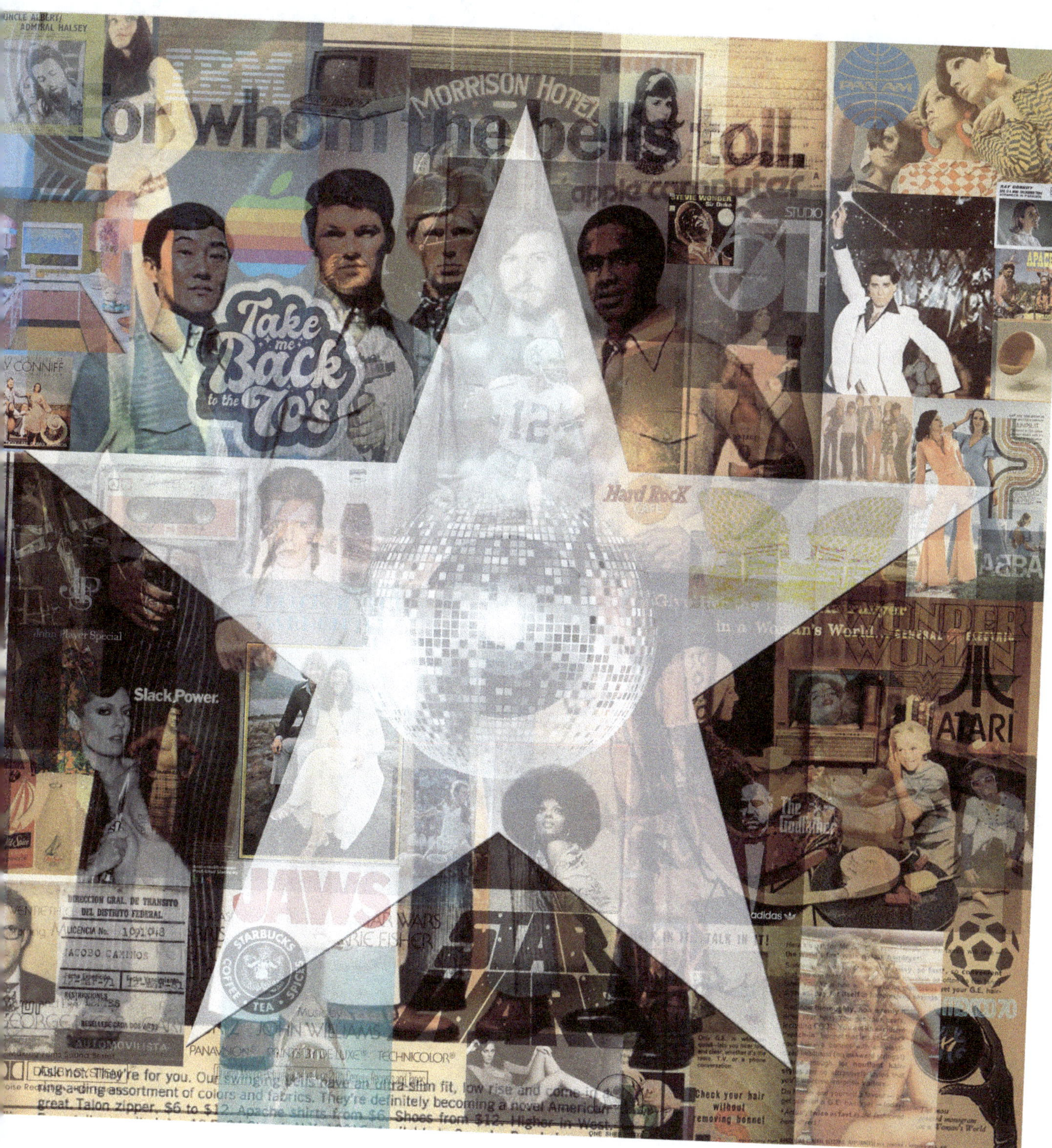

Februllage 2022

Mixed Media
Técnica Mixta
Feb 2022

FABIÁN GILES

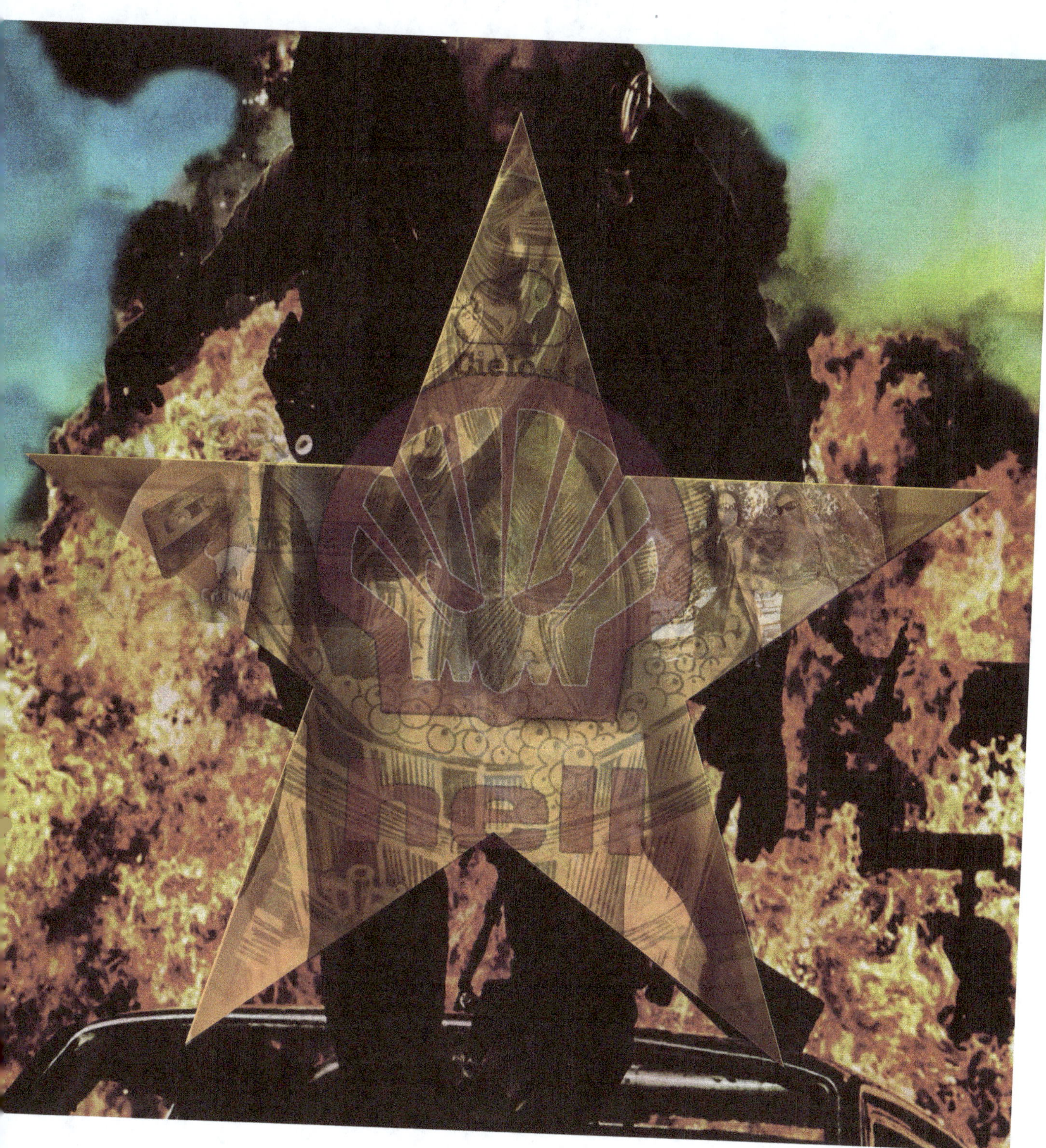

Februllage 2022

27 The Highest Mountains

Mixed Media
Técnica Mixta
Feb 2022

FABIÁN GILES

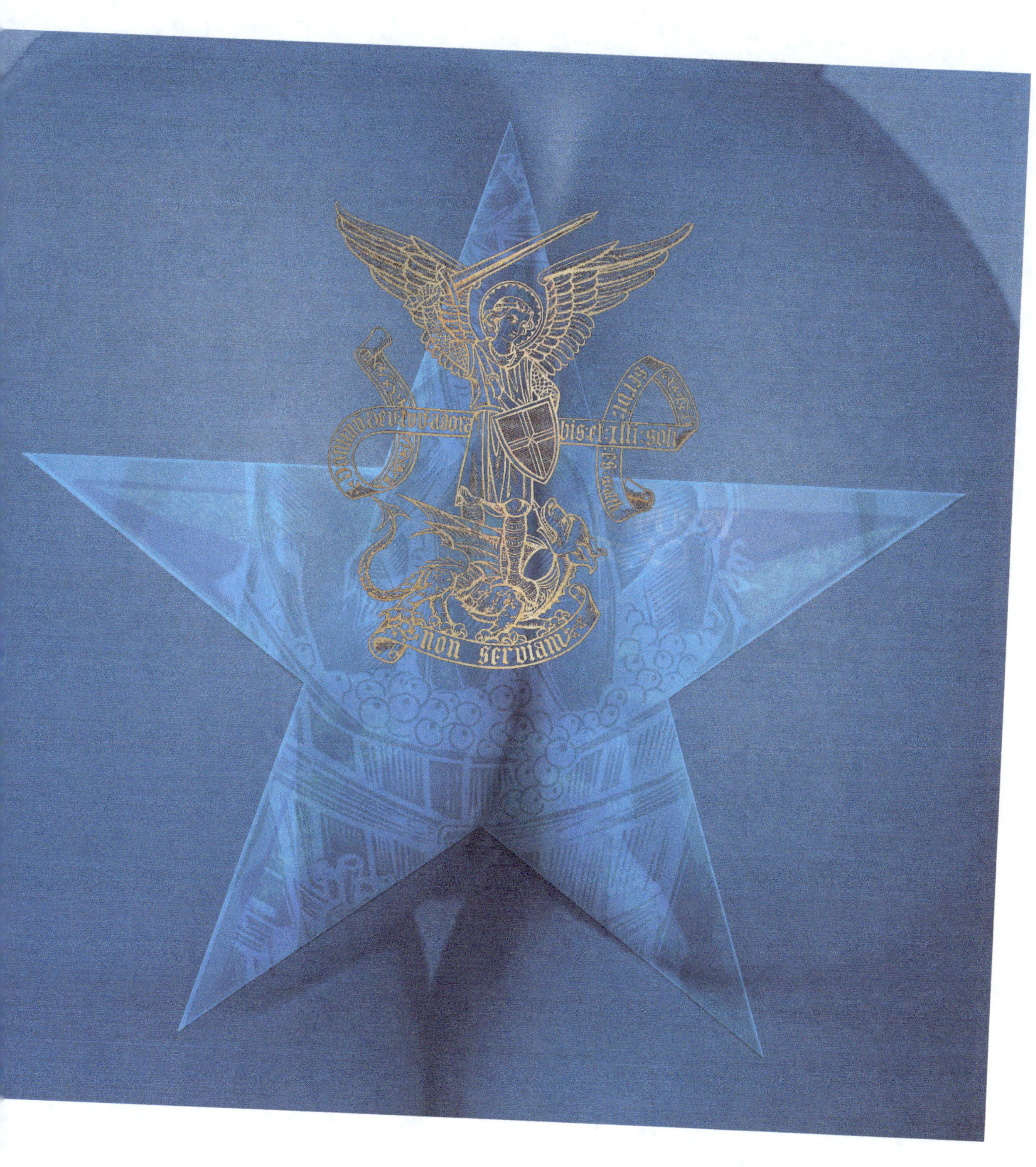

Februllage 2022

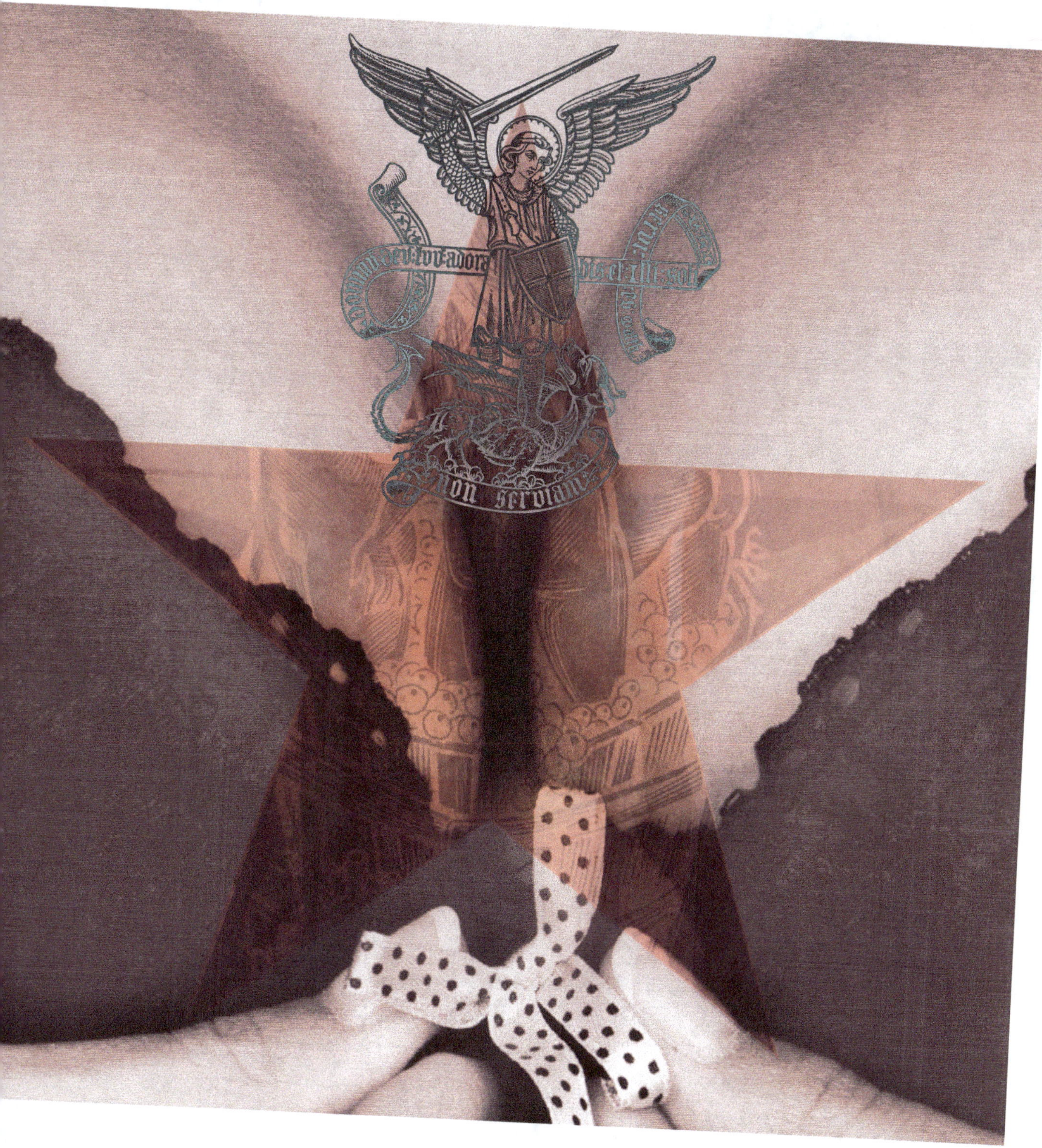
non serviam

Februllage 2022

28 Tijeras
Mixed Media
Técnica Mixta
Feb 2022

FABIÁN GILES

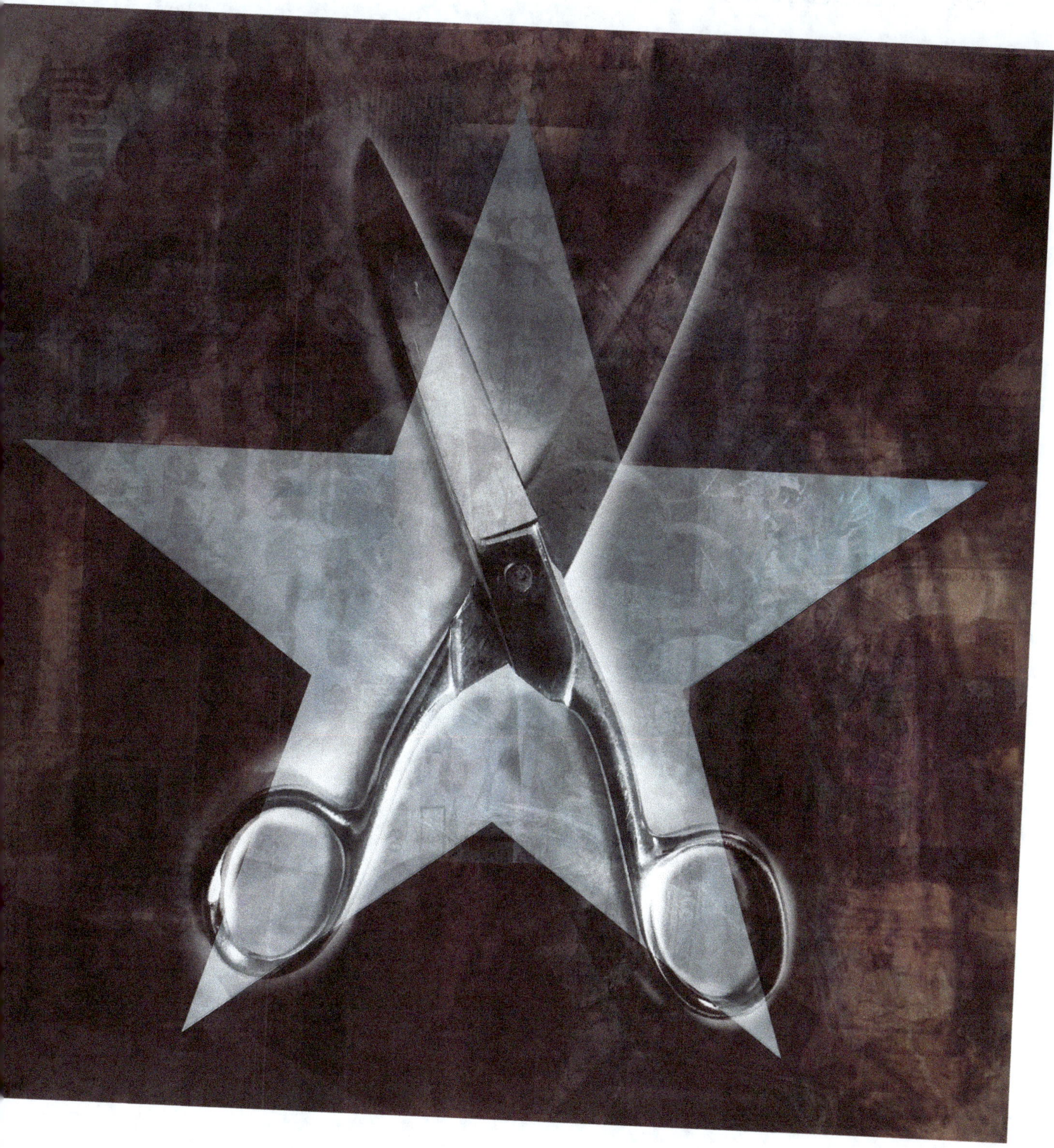

Acknowledgements
Agradecimientos

Edinburgh Collage Collective

The Scandinavian Collage Museum

Kolaj Magazine

Sebastián Reséndiz

Paco, Bob y Richie Giles

Carlos Pérez Bucio

Héctor Pineda

Óscar Palos

César Martínez Silva

Miguel Ángel Corona

Pedro Meyer

Jonás González

Juan Carlos Molar

Margarita Jair

Carolina Amor

Daiana Sanzo

Cecilia Yañez

Dahlia Azul

Jessica Aldama

See you on / Nos vemos en

Februllage 2023

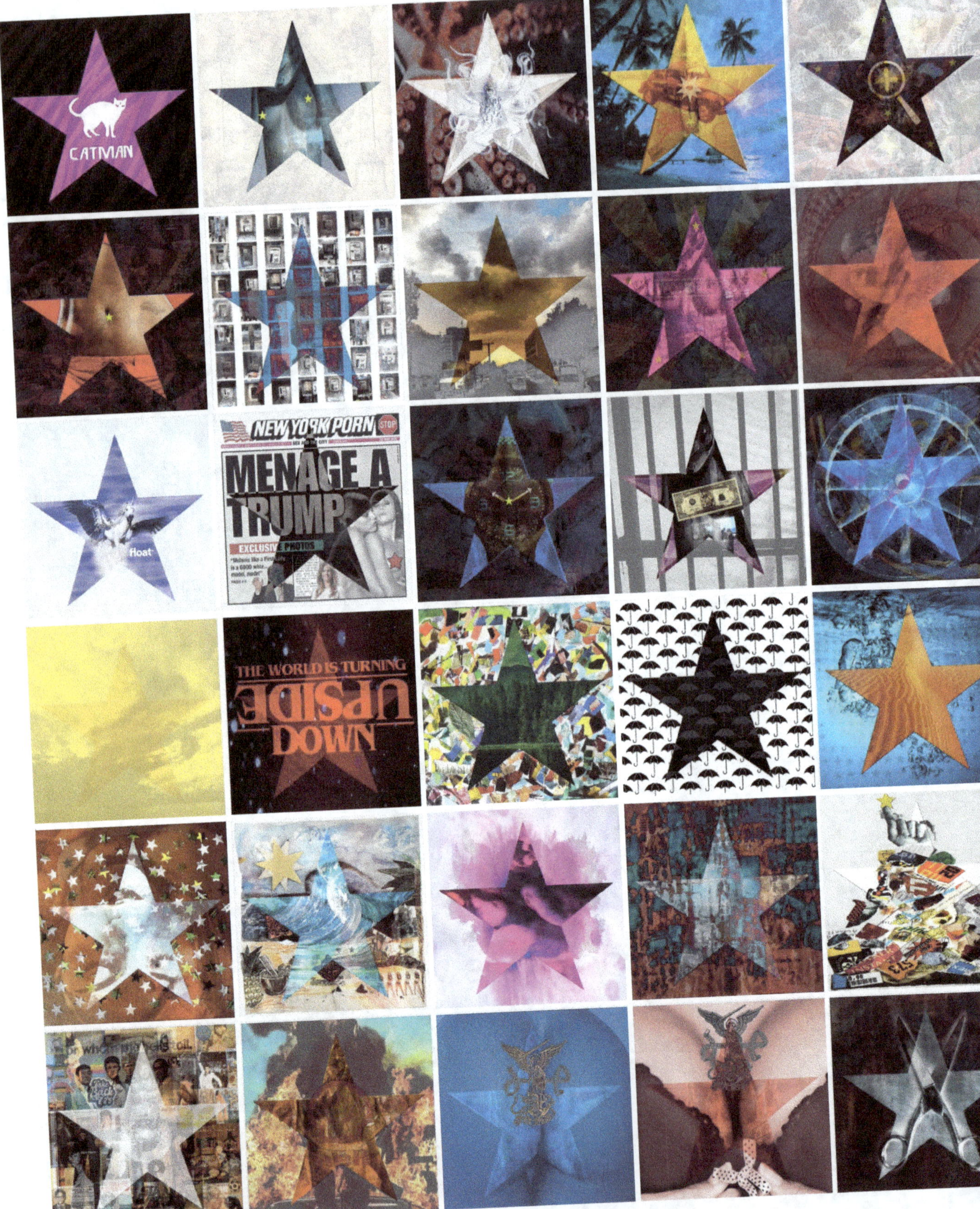

*All these artworks are
available on* Saatchi Art

Todas estas obras están
disponibles en Saatchi Art

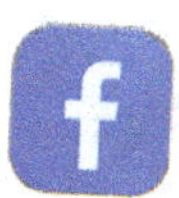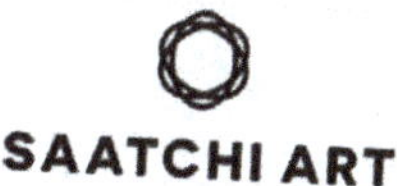

FABIANGILES   WWW.SAATCHIART.COM/FABIANGILES